Exploring the
LANCASTER CANAL

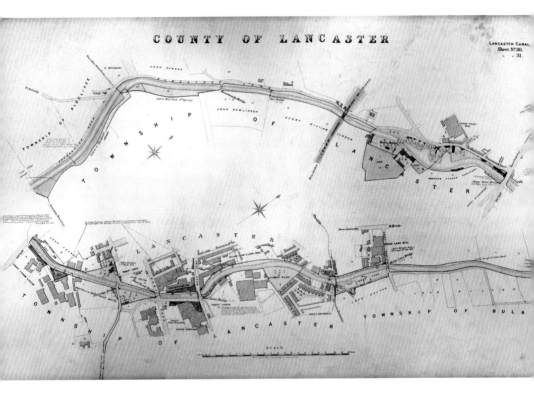

Courtesy of Lancaster Maritime Museum

Exploring the
LANCASTER CANAL
a history and guide

ROBERT SWAIN

First published in 2019
by Palatine Books, Carnegie House, Chatsworth
Road, Lancaster LA1 4SL
www.carnegiepublishing.com

British Library Cataloguing-in-Publication data
A catalogue record for this book is available from
the British Library

ISBN 13: 978-1-910837-22-1

Designed and typeset by
Carnegie Book Production

Printed and bound by Cambrian Printers

Contents

Foreword

THIS IS A BRAND NEW, TOTALLY revised, considerably enlarged incar-
nation of a previous book, *A Walker's Guide to the Lancaster Canal*,
published over 30 years ago. At that time, a link with the main canal
system was just a dream. We now have the Millennium Ribble Link.

Over the years there have been many changes on the Lancaster Canal,
as will be seen in this book. During my boyhood there were very few
boats passing along, cruising not then being as popular as it is today.
There are now several marinas that did not exist until more recent times.
Cyclists could not use the towpath when the first edition was published.
It is to reflect these changes, and the hugely increased popularity of the
canal, that this new book came into being. No doubt there will be many
changes to come, hopefully for the benefit of the canal and all those who
derive pleasure from it.

The book does not claim to be a complete history. There are many
gaps in its story as things which were looked upon as commonplace at
the time and went unremarked would now be of real historical interest.
Therefore all opinions expressed and conclusions drawn are my own;
further information could, as always, come to light to prove or disprove
them at a later stage.

Measurements are kept in the old system as that is the way they are in
old canal documents. There were eight furlongs in a mile, so five furlongs
were roughly a kilometre. A kilometre is roughly five-eighths of a mile. A
metre is roughly one and one-tenth yards.

When the canal was built and in regular commercial use the currency
was in pounds, shillings and pence. Even the pence could be quartered.
To help younger readers with no experience of old money, the pound
was split into twenty shillings and shillings were split into twelve pence,
making for 240 pence to the pound. In current decimal figures we have:

    1 shilling = 5 pence
    2 shillings = 10 pence
    3 shillings = 15 pence

4 shillings = 20 pence
5 shillings = 25 pence
6 shillings = 30 pence
7 shillings = 35 pence
8 shillings = 40 pence
9 shillings = 45 pence
10 shillings = 50 pence
15 shillings = 75 pence

2.4 pence = 1 penny
4.8 pence = 2 pence
7.2 pence = 3 pence
9.6 pence = 4 pence
12.0 pence = 1 shilling.

If a figure quoted in the book was 7 shillings and 10 pence (7/10), this becomes 35 pence plus 4 pence as the nearest equivalent, that is 39 pence. Something which is 16 shillings and 2 pence (16/2) becomes 80 pence plus one penny as the nearest equivalent, or 81 pence.

Reference is also made to guineas. A guinea was £1 1s. 0d., or £1.05. Guineas were regularly quoted for professional fees.

Hollowforth Aqueduct

PART ONE

The Canal Story

Marshalls or Six Mile Bridge

CHAPTER 1

Conception and Construction

THE LANCASTER CANAL IS A CHILD of the canal fever of the 1700s whose promotion came largely from Lancaster itself. In those times Lancaster was a more important town than Preston and a competitor as a port with Liverpool. Communications were bad, so much so that it was actually cheaper to import foreign goods to the town than to bring English goods from places such as Wigan and Manchester! Roads were in a terrible condition; according to an account of 1768 by the topographer Arthur Young, between Preston and Wigan there were ruts 4 feet deep floating with mud. He passed three carts which had broken down. Tongue in cheek he wrote that, in winter 'it would have cost no more money to make the roads navigable than to make them hard.' Perhaps a bit of an exaggerated claim, but still giving an impression of conditions.

The constantly shifting sands of the tidal Lune made Lancaster a difficult port to enter. The original port at Sunderland Point on the north side of the estuary was superseded by the construction of St. George's Quay just below the town. Glasson Dock was finished 5 miles further down the Lune in 1787, complete with a fully equipped wet dock. However the sandbanks of the outer estuary still had to be negotiated, so, in 1799 a scheme was promoted to build a new dock at Thornbush which, with the aid of a canal through into Lancaster would replace Glasson Dock. Thornbush was about a quarter of a mile north of Crook Farm at the end of the saltmarsh. This scheme would have overcome the silting problems but was abandoned because the West India trade declined.

Coal reached Lancaster and the surrounding district by sea from the River Douglas, making it an expensive commodity. The same supply line served the Kendal area through the port of Milnthorpe at the mouth of the River Bela on the Kent estuary. At that time both south Westmorland and north Lancashire had a plentiful supply of limestone to be burnt into the agricultural lime required for use in arable country further south. This was the background against which the Lancaster Canal was conceived. These two products led to the Lancaster Canal being known as 'The Black and White Canal'.

Originally it was proposed that a canal be built from a junction with the Leeds–Liverpool Canal at Walton-le-Dale, through Preston and Lancaster to Kendal. In the late 1760s it was further suggested that this line be continued from Walton to Worsley, near Manchester, where it would join the Bridgewater Canal, England's first modern canal. At a meeting held at Lancaster town hall on 13 November 1771, which proposed a canal northwards from the Leeds and Liverpool, it was decided that a survey should be made. James Brindley was approached and commenced the survey but had to relinquish the task to his pupil Robert Whitworth owing to ill health. Whitworth put forward a plan in 1772 for a canal from the proposed Leeds and Liverpool near Eccleston, crossing the Ribble below Penwortham Bridge, travelling over the Fylde Plain almost to Kirkham, then back eastwards nearly to Barton and finally north again. The Lune crossing was to be below Skerton Bridge at Lancaster. The long level of 54.5 miles terminated at Tewitfield to the north of Carnforth where there was to be a rise of 86 feet, the remaining 18 miles to Kendal being level again.

This line did not satisfy the committee who asked Whitworth to try to find an easier Lune crossing. He took a higher line, locking up 24 feet from the Ribble at Sidegreave. From there the course was to Salwick Hall, then eastward again to Hough where it turned north to pass to the east of Garstang and Lancaster with a long hair-pin bend nearly to Halton, and from there on to Tewitfield, a grand total of 55.5 miles. He observed that 'notwithstanding the 24 feet rise, this was the easier and better line.' At Tewitfield a rise of 62 feet was necessary and the line there followed a very similar line to the canal's existing course through Holme, Farleton, Crooklands and Hincaster Tunnel to Kendal. All this was, of course, done without the aid of modern surveying instruments. The committee was still not satisfied and sought further advice on easier ways to cross the Ribble and the Lune, one of which was by taking a line as far up as Halton Scars. Each surveyor came to the conclusion that it was necessary to drop to Whitworth's line. A major objection to the scheme was that the course did not extend far enough south to reach the Wigan coalfields.

In 1781 there was a survey made for a canal from Ingleton and Burton-in-Lonsdale to join the Lune at or near Lancaster, but it came to nothing.

A further scheme was put forward by John Wilkinson, the ironmaster of Castlehead near Lindale. His scheme, probably originated with John Jenkinson of Yealand, was to enclose and drain 18,710 acres of Morecambe Bay at a cost of £150,000. John Longbotham, who surveyed the scheme, proposed closing the sands and building a channel from the River Winster where it entered the Kent Estuary, across Foulshaw Moss to Nether

Levens. Here it would join the River Kent which would be diverted along the coast to Arnside. It would then cut through the isthmus to join the coast again near Warton Crag and follow the coastline to Heysham Head where it could enter the sea. The channel was to be navigable from the Kent to Bare where a short canal would be cut across the Lune almost opposite Lancaster. Presumably there was insufficient support for the idea as nothing came of this one either.

1791 saw patience running short. By then it was considered to be a matter of necessity to Kendal, Lancaster and perhaps Preston to get on a footing with their southern neighbours or to submit to a decline in their trade and population. On 4 June 1791 twenty-nine prominent merchants and traders of Lancaster presented a petition to the mayor, asking him to convene a public meeting to consider making a canal and linking it with the Leeds and Liverpool. The petition set forth the advantages held by their rival port of Liverpool as a result of having inland navigation:

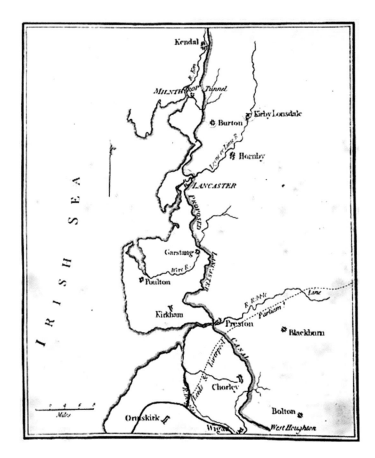

Proposed route of the Lancaster Canal, from canalrivertrust.org.uk.

The advantages the town of Liverpool has derived from their inland navigations, and so much increased from the progress of the Canal towards Leeds, which is going forward with great spirit. The completion whereof and those projected cutts [*sic*] to Bury, Bolton, etc. which are in agitation with little doubt of success, will add further benefit, and give the merchants and traders in that place so decided a superiority in the vend of their imports as greatly to diminish the commerce of this town, and its consequences, materially affect the landed interest in the neighbourhood, unless some means can be found to meet them in the market upon more equal terms.

The outcome of the resultant public meeting on 8 June was a resolution to promote a canal and a subscription list was opened.

Samuel Gregson of Lancaster was appointed as clerk. Longbotham, Robert Dickinson of Gargrave and Richard Beck were, during the next few months, asked to resurvey Whitworth's line and also extend it southwards at Worsley, but were unable to find a better alternative.

Canal and remains of Greenhalgh Castle

In October 1791 John Rennie, the engineer, was asked to make a survey, the committee being undecided whether to make for the Manchester, Bolton and Bury Canal or the Bridgewater Canal. His terms were that he should be paid two guineas (£2.10) per day plus expenses for his work. Rennie worked fast during the December of that year and the January of 1792 and came up with a plan for a broad canal which was accepted. The line was to commence at Westhoughton, situated in the coalfield midway between Bolton and Wigan, thus making a canal of twice the value to the districts it would serve. It was to continue on the level for 15.5 miles to Clayton Green, lock down 222 feet in a flight of thirty-two locks to an embankment across the Ribble Valley, then cross the river by aqueduct to Preston. Beyond this, Whitworth's upper line was to be followed as far as the Calder where Rennie desired a branch to go round the north side of Greenhalgh Castle to Garstang, cross the Wyre by an aqueduct, then join the line again at Cabus Nook. At Ashton, to the south of Lancaster, there was to be a deep cutting and the Lune would be crossed further downstream. The canal would then travel onwards to Tewitfield, a level 42.5 miles. Here he proposed a flight of five locks, with another four near Milton where he rejoined Whitworth's line, making a total rise of 65 feet. In order that the canal could serve Wakefield's gunpowder mills at Sedgwick it was still necessary to tunnel through Hincaster Hill. A further 5 miles took the canal to Kendal, making a total length of 75.5 miles. In addition Rennie added two branches to the main line, one from Chorley to Duxbury (3 miles) and the other from Tewitfield to Warton Crag (2.5 miles), neither of which was ever constructed in the end.

A General Meeting was held in Lancaster town hall on 7 February 1792 when it was 'Resolved unanimously that a subscription should be entered into for obtaining an Act of Parliament to carry the said canal into execution and the defraying all expenses necessary for completing same.' £247,800 is said to have been promised before the meeting terminated, a sum which had risen to £370,500 before the end of the month.

By now it was essential that an Act of Parliament was obtained as soon as possible as the Leeds and Liverpool Canal backers were proposing to alter their line to one nearly parallel to the Lancaster one between Whittle-le-Woods and Wigan. Negotiations took place between the Lancaster committee and those for the Leeds and Liverpool, and the Manchester, Bolton and Bury canals. However, opposition to the Lancaster's Bill failed and it was passed by Parliament on 25 June 1792, authorising Rennie's line and branches and junctions with possible future canals (which were never constructed) from the Fylde, Hornby, Ingleton and Kirkby Lonsdale. Water was to be taken from the River Mint at Mintsfeet,

Kendal, provision being made for mill owners to draw, if necessary, from the canal provided that its level did not drop to less than 5 feet. The authorised share capital was £414,000 divided into £100 shares. £60,000 was to be set aside solely for the Westmorland section. Additionally, permission was given to borrow an extra £200,000 if needed. Duties on coal were fixed at 2s. 3d. per ton (maximum) descending the locks to the Ribble and not proceeding more than 18 miles north of Chorley, with 1½d. per ton/mile elsewhere.

Amongst the petitioners for the canal were John Dilworth (who was elected chairman of the Lancaster Canal Navigation at the first meeting of the proprietors on 3 July 1792) and Thomas Worswick (elected treasurer), both bankers of Lancaster. John Brockbank, a Lancaster shipbuilder, the Earl of Balcarres, a coal owner, John Wakefield and Thomas Crewdson of Kendal and further prominent people of the two towns were other petitioners.

The canal committee was formed mainly of Lancaster men, there being only one each from Preston and Kendal. They appointed John Rennie engineer in July 1792 at £600 p.a. He was required to reside at Lancaster for five months a year and give attendance as requested at other times. The appointment of assistant surveyor went to William Crosley of Brighouse, whilst in 1793 Archibald Millar of Dublin was appointed resident engineer and superintendent.

The committee wasted no time in commencing the construction of the canal. The first contract, dated 31 December 1792, was awarded to John Pinkerton, well known as a canal contractor, and John Murray of Colne. This was for the section from Ellel Grange to Tewitfield and was for £52,000, exclusive of bridges and culverts. The second contract, awarded in 1793, was for Ellel to Ray Lane near Catterall, making a total of 27 miles which, as experience was to show, was much too long a stretch.

In order to outflank the Leeds and Liverpool, it was essential to start work south of Preston and in July 1793, the length from Bark Hill near Wigan to Adlington near Chorley was let to Paul Vickers of Thorne.

It was decided at the first annual shareholders' meeting in January 1793 that communication with the sea was desirable, the outcome being Rennie's proposed branch from Galgate to Glasson Dock. This was authorised by a second Act of 10 May 1793. This Act also imposed further restrictions on the drawing of water from the Lune, the Wyre and from mines near Heapey which were adjacent to the Leeds and Liverpool's parliamentary line. Water, if required, was to be provided free elsewhere by mines within 2,000 yards of the canal, provided that it didn't have to be pumped from the pithead.

Negotiations were successfully concluded with the Duke of Bridgewater to extend the Lancaster Canal from Westhoughton to his own canal at Worsley, at a cost estimated by Rennie to be £63,544. A Bill authorising the connection was promoted in 1794 but lost, mainly owing to opposition by Miss Henrietta Atherton of Atherton Hall. The Duke decided to build a branch to Leigh and the Bill was not revived, the Lancaster committee feeling that the new branch might be more suitable for their junction in any case.

Meanwhile wrangling continued with the Manchester, Bolton and Bury and the Leeds and Liverpool Committees over the latter's proposed deviation to the south of the Ribble. In October 1793 the Lancaster committee suggested that the Leeds and Liverpool join their line near Heapey, where both lines became parallel, which would have destroyed the Leeds and Liverpool's level to the Manchester, Bolton and Bury Canal. In turn the Leeds and Liverpool counter-proposed that the Lancaster should strike south-eastwards, abandoning their own line and joining the Leeds and Liverpool at Newburgh. Access to the Bridgewater could then be from a branch of the Leeds and Liverpool at Wigan, attracting some Liverpool–Manchester traffic.

This second plan was not acceptable to the Lancaster committee, who were aware that their rival lacked funds, and was also opposed by the Duke of Bridgewater. Work on their south level had already been started and was supported by both the Duke and the Wigan coal owners.

However, a deviation was badly needed by the Leeds and Liverpool and to succeed they needed the backing of the Manchester, Bolton and Bury and the Lancaster. Inevitably a compromise with the Lancaster was reached. In April 1794, they agreed to support the deviation (and also the Manchester, Bolton and Bury's extension Bill) in return for support for a small deviation at Cabus, near Garstang, and the Worsley extension. There would now be two parallel lines, enabling the Leeds and Liverpool at Heapey to ensure that traffic would pass over their canal to the Bridgewater. If the junction was not built, there was the proviso that the Lancaster would pay the Leeds and Liverpool 1*d.* per ton for all goods which would have passed through it on the way to Manchester, taking the shortest route. The Leeds and Liverpool's Bill was passed on 9 May 1794 but, as has been seen, the Lancaster's was rejected.

Construction of the canal was proceeding whilst the various wranglings and negotiations took place, but not so quickly as it might have done. Pinkerton and Murray had not always been present to supervise the work as they were often attending to contracts on other canals. Not all the work was done by their own men, but various works were let to subcontractors for the lowest possible price. Workmen were allowed to wander onto land which had not been purchased by the Lancaster Canal Navigation (but referred to as Lancaster Canal Company from here for ease of understanding). Archibald Millar, the resident engineer, frequently complained of their inattention and bad workmanship. He found that Pinkerton and Murray ignored his instructions as soon as he had left an area, sometimes digging the canal yards from the line which he had laid.

During the building of the canal, various sections were completed and filled with water to enable boats to transport materials from one area to another. Once filled with water, it was not possible for Millar to check the puddle lining the canal to see that it had been properly made. Pinkerton and Murray objected to his wish to have those sections drained to be able to make his inspection.

In 1796 things came to a head between Millar and the contractors. Whitworth, the assistant surveyor, was called in to arbitrate. As a result the Lancaster Canal Company took over the disputed works in September and let them again as single lots under Millar's supervision. There were thirty-five contractors between Borwick and Preston, all having short stretches of perhaps two bridges or 500 yards of the line each. Millar was then able to supervise the construction of the canal to his satisfaction.

In their first detailed report published on 30 August 1795, the committee reported that it was hoped to complete the Tewitfield to Ellel Grange section within two years, much of the masonry work on the bridges and aqueducts being well advanced. The section from Ellel Grange to the River Calder it was hoped, would be completed in sixteen months, whilst the section on to Myerscough Wood should be completed in eighteen months. The parliamentary line had a considerable quantity of deep cutting. To save time and money, agreements had been made for a deviation of the line. Nothing further appears to have been done north of the Ribble. To the south of the river, work was almost complete on the section from Limebrick Beck (near Chorley) to Bark Hill, but had been held up by long and severe frosts the previous winter. That length would be completed shortly.

In 1794 Henry Eastburn had been appointed as resident engineer to the section south of the Ribble, with Thomas Fletcher assisting. Bark Hill to Addlington, a stretch of 4.5 miles, was opened in 1795. Enough work had been done by July 1796 to allow a little coal traffic to commence, earning some badly needed revenue.

The French Wars were causing hardship and restricting the flow of capital. Share calls were being ignored by some of the shareholders and the company was heavily in debt with the treasurer's bank. An appeal for further subscriptions in advance met with little success, but a second appeal in 1797 was more forthcoming.

Open country near Park Head Bridge

In May 1796, a third Act was obtained to authorise the purchase of some lands from the Duchy of Lancaster for a small deviation at Myerscough. During this same year plans for extending the line of the canal to Kendal were shelved and the Westmorland proprietors began to get restless (mainly because of the proposal to appropriate the statutory reserve of £60,000 reserved for the northern section in order to finance current work).

By now the Preston to Tewitfield section was almost completed, apart from the Lune aqueduct which was started in January 1794 but not completed until autumn 1797. More will be said about this magnificent structure later.

On 22 November 1797, the Lancaster Canal was formally opened from Spital Moss, just outside Preston, to Tewitfield. A cavalcade of six boats took part in the ceremony, but the actual voyage was only from Lancaster to the aqueduct and back. The order of proceedings was drawn up in great detail:

> The Committee meet in the office in Lancaster at 9.30 a.m. are to proceed from there, accompanied with colours and music, to the Canal Bridge in the Fryerage, where the boats must be placed ready to receive them in the following order.
>
> Committee Barge. Committee, Leeds and Liverpool Committee and the most respectable of the landowners. The 'Bee' and 'Ceres' are to be fitted up for the particular friends of the Committee and the most respectable persons in Lancaster. Two of the trading boats belonging to the Company and the 'Elephant' are to be fitted up for the Proprietors in general and are to follow in order.

There is much more instruction including how, if the day be favourable, the notables may step out and view the aqueduct whilst the boats were turning, the order of the boats for the return, where the band was to sail and the composition of the procession to the Kings Arms Hotel in Market Street, Lancaster, to dine. Volleys were to be fired at various points, the final one in front of the town hall (which was then in Market Street and is now the City Museum).

In 1797 the 4 mile stretch from Adlington to Knowley Wharf, near Chorley, was opened. The balance sheet for the first six years to 1 December 1798 gives details of the expenditure incurred during the construction of the Lancaster Canal. Summarised, these were:

Lancaster Level:

Land etc.	42,604	17	1½
General constructional expenditure	178,158	11	2
Lune aqueduct	48,320	18	10
Hydraulic Pozzolano earth from Italy	321	8	9
	269,405	15	10½

Wigan Level:

Land etc.	5,760	1	6
General constructional expenditure	55,416	16	3½
	61,176	17	9½

Not particularly applicable to either part:

Applications to Parliament	6,327	1	2
Salaries, fees etc.	16,341	11	9
Quarrying, boat building etc.	1,803	10	8
Interest to proprietors	27,510	12	9
	51,892	16	4
	£382,565	10	0

These figures were calculated after deducting sales and interest received.

By 1799 William Cartwright was resident engineer to the Lancaster Canal Company (he had been assistant resident engineer since January 1794 with a salary of £250 p.a., and had come from Basingstoke), as Millar's and Eastburn's contracts were not renewed. He reported to the committee that the South End from Bark Hill to Johnson's Hillock (12 miles) and that the remaining part to Clayton Green was well advanced, apart from the Whittle Hill's tunnel.

Until now the Company had suffered from financial difficulties, response from the proprietors having been poor; in July 1798 there was only £6,500 in the hands of the committee. Receipts from Tonnage from 1 December 1797 to 1 December 1798 amounted to just over £2,002, which was to be apportioned in the payment of interest, salaries, etc. However, a time of expansion now started, canalside industry continuing to grow until the railway era in the 1840s. On the North End the Company started a packet-boat service in August 1798, between Preston and Lancaster, run by two boats which were to be paid for from their own earnings. By the end of the 1798 year, the Committee reported there was a total revenue of £2,022, with £1,616 from the Lancaster Level and £406 from the South End.

At the 1 January 1799 General Meeting the Committee reported that Tonnage for the last quarter to 1 December 1798 was nearly equal to the total for the three previous quarters, and that was in spite of a stoppage to the north of Lancaster for three weeks owing to a breach in the Lune embankment. At that time £3,314 11s. 7d. was owing to the contractors.

An adjourned General Meeting was held on 29 January 1799 to discuss raising monies to pay debts, and was to call a sum not exceeding £15 per share. The Committee was directed that 'they shall not proceed in the extension of the Line or any other Works further than they will be able to do by the said fifteen Pounds per share.' That was to be paid in three instalments of £5 in March, July and October 1799. The Minute prohibiting the further extension of the canal was rescinded at the 1 July 1800 General Meeting.

Samuel Gregson and three other committee members, trading as Samuel Gregson and Company, built lime-kilns at Preston and the Canal company opened up quarries. Between Bark Hill and Chorley in the following years new pits from the Lancaster were opened, numerous lime-kilns were built at both ends of the canal, cinder ovens were built in the Tewitfield area (to provide a fluxing agent for the charcoal iron smelting of Lonsdale) and coke ovens were erected near Carnforth. See chapter ten for more about coke ovens. There was coal traffic from small local pits in the Farleton area as well as from the mining areas at the southern end of the canal.

CHAPTER 2

Ribble Problems
and through to Kendal

B Y NOW THE MAIN PROBLEM was the connection of the two ends of the
canal across the Ribble. Owing to bad roads at Johnson's Hillock,
coal from collieries close to the South End near Wigan was being carted
to the Douglas, sailed from there to Preston and then carted again to
the North End. Various proposals were considered in 1796 and 1797 for
a branch canal from the North End at Salwick to Savock, followed by
an inclined plane down to the Ribble. An alternative was for a tramroad
from Tulketh, nearer Preston, when traffic could then be exchanged with
the Douglas, which the Leeds and Liverpool agreed to improve, but the
Lancaster had insufficient funds for the financing of this work. Even more
expensive was the building of an aqueduct which had been considered in
1794; Rennie estimated that the cost of a three-arched structure of 116
feet a span, plus embankments, was £94,979.

Cartwright was asked to make a survey and on 1 November 1799 the
committee issued a report of his findings. He said that the south level
was intended to terminate at Clayton Green, the most northerly point
before the commencement to the general fall to the vale of the Ribble. He
estimated the cost of locking down 222 feet and then crossing the Ribble
by an aqueduct at £180,945. Instead, as a cheaper and simpler method,
he advised a double wagonway (one road for ascending and the other for
descending wagons) to be hauled by a stationary steam engine. The river
was to be crossed by a wooden bridge, then a similar wagonway was to
be built to a proposed basin at Preston, requiring a short extension of
the North End from Spital Moss. The estimated cost was £60,000. To
finance this, and also pay off the debts of the Company, a fourth Act of
Parliament was obtained in 1800 which granted the power to raise an
additional £200,000 in £30 shares.

Not all the monies were payable at once. An advert in the *Lancaster
Gazette* for 20 June 1801 requested 'respective proprietors of New Shares
to pay Thomas Worswick £5 per share in cash or Bank of England notes

Mute swans, Salwick

before 1st, July 1801', this being for the third call. A further £5 per New Share was called to be paid by 1 October 1801, and this was to continue every quarter until the shares had been paid in full.

A Mr Monk, who was probably a Leeds and Liverpool committee man, now came onto the scene with a further proposal to join the Leeds and Liverpool Canal. He considered Cartwright's tramroad good but expensive. His own suggestion was that the Douglas Navigation be continued from Rufford, via Tarleton Bridge and Bank Hall to Penwortham where it would lock down to the Ribble. An inclined plane could be built up to the Lancaster and the Leeds and Liverpool from Haigh to Wigan, this being by lock. This circuitous route, Monk estimated, would require an extra four hours time compared with Cartwright's tramroad when taking coal from Chorley to Preston. As compensation he suggested that the Leeds and Liverpool's tolls be reduced by 6d. a ton.

As has been mentioned, a number of the Lancaster proprietors owned coal mines between Wigan and Chorley. One of them, Alexander Haliburton from Haigh, in a long letter to George Clayton dated 25 February 1800, claimed that the scheme was a bait to the Lancaster's coal owners and that Mr Monk's real intention was to enrich the Leeds and Liverpool Canal at the expense of the Lancaster. He estimated that the Company would lose £54,100 in the first year and £10,750 annually thereafter if it was adopted, and was of the firm opinion that Cartwright's plan was preferable. He also said that there would be other disadvantages arising from the uncertainty of sailing across the Ribble. His estimate was that a ton of coal delivered at Lancaster would cost 12s. 11d. with Cartwright's plan, but 16s. 7d. with Monk's. In conclusion he wrote that

> the North End would be from thence supplied with a much greater proportion of the trade than has been calculated upon, and should it never go further, the views of the Company would be more amply fulfilled than by falling in with the insidious proposals of their Leeds and Liverpool rivals.

Not surprisingly, with the conflicting views, the committee asked John Rennie, their original engineer, and William Jessop to survey and give their opinion on the schemes. (Jessop was an experienced engineer of canals, having built a number particularly in the North East and the Midlands, who was completing the Rochdale Canal at the time. He also had practical experience in the building of tramroads.) Their report to the committee was presented to the General Meeting on 7 July 1801. They said, 'We are still of the opinion that an embankment to the full height of the Lancaster level, and a Stone Aqueduct will be most advisable', this being together with locks up to Clayton Green. If the company was prepared to go to 'extraordinary expense', the work could be done in three years, otherwise five. Attached to their report was a design for the aqueduct. It was to be built of stone, be 640 feet in length, have three elliptical arches with a span of 116 feet each 57 feet in height from the low water mark to the towing path. The cost was to be less than £94,979. There were two other designs for an aqueduct. One, from Cartwright, was for a slightly shorter aqueduct with three spans of 120 feet each, which was to incorporate Corinthian pilasters. The other design, by Thomas Gibson, was for a continuous aqueduct with pointed arches, three of which were to span the Ribble. There were to be cross arches between the main spans and an immense pediment (a triangular piece with a long base). Rennie and Jessop, knowing that the Lancaster Canal Company did not have the funds available to build an aqueduct, approved Cartwright's tramroad, which it was estimated would cost £21,600, as a temporary measure. Owing to the advantage it would give to the Leeds and Liverpool they condemned the Douglas scheme. Cartwright's scheme for the building of the tramroad was immediately adopted and Jessop was retained to survey the Preston end of the line. For the work and the survey Jessop was paid £70, and £112 5s. 4d. was credited to Rennie's account.

No time was lost in starting the work which involved the cutting of the 259-yard tunnel through Whittle Hill to complete the line to Clayton Green, constructing a further mile of canal to Walton Summit which was the tramroad terminus, building the tramroad itself and extending the North End by half a mile into Preston. A basin was to be built to the north of Fishergate. Instead of the one year antici-pated by Cartwright, it in fact took two years to bore the tunnel. The January 1803 General Meeting reported that the rail road had been very much retarded by the contractors not finishing the cast iron rails in accordance with agreement. On 1 June 1803 the first boat passed through to Walton Summit where its cargo of coal was transhipped to tramroad wagons. However, the tramroad was only finished to Bamber Bridge and was not completed through to Preston until the end of the year. Its route skirted Avenham Brow, behind what is now Ribblesdale Place, and turned due north, passing under Fishergate (the tunnel is now access to a car park) to the wharf. The tramroad had a double track for ascending and descending wagons and three inclined planes worked by stationary engines and endless chains, one of which rose from the then wooden trestle bridge in Avenham Park. Although this bridge over the Ribble has been rebuilt several times, it is still known as 'The Old Tram Bridge' today.

To help finance the completion of the works, it was resolved on 2 August 1803 that the Proprietors be asked to loan £3 for each share held, for which interest would be paid at five per cent per annum until the loan was repaid.

Shortly after the tramroad was completed, on 19 January 1804, Cartwright died, probably as a result of overwork. During his time as an engineer to the Lancaster Canal he had planned and supervised the cutting of a tunnel from the canal at Preston, through the rock and out into the Ribble, the water being pumped to the canal by a Boulton and Watt steam engine. The work was completed by William Miller of Preston, an assistant engineer for some years, with pumping commencing in July 1806.

Another of Cartwright's schemes had been taking water from the River Keer at Capernwray Mill, to pump the water into the canal. In the event the pump was not built, owing to opposition from the mill owners, but a feeder from the river was cut. One of Cartwright's final designs was for a 2,200 yard tramroad from Tewitfield to the quarries at Kellet Seeds, but this, also, was not built. It is thought that the bay on the towpath side of the canal here was ready for the branch.

The opening of the tramroad had an immediate effect on the Company's revenue. For 1803 gross income was £4,853, whilst for 1804, after the tramroad opened, it rose to £8,490. In 1803 a first dividend of ½ per cent was declared. The second dividend declared was 1 per cent in 1805, a rate that continued unchanged until 1825. (An analysis of revenue from 1807 is listed in Table 2.)

As the length of the South End, including the tramroad, was only 19 miles (compared with 42 miles for the North End to Tewitfield) the major part of the traffic was clearly being discharged at Preston. So Preston began to assume a greater importance than Lancaster in the affairs of the canal, although it was still in the control of men from the latter town.

The Westmorland proprietors were by this time becoming justifiably restless because of the continued deferment of the completion of the line from Tewitfield to Kendal. At last, in 1805, the Company began considering the continuation of the canal. William Miller made surveys for two routes to Kendal: one was via Hincaster with a 340 yard tunnel through Hincaster Hill, the other was shorter but had a tunnel of 670 yards at Raines Hall, Sedgwick. As an alternative he suggested a 13-mile tramroad from Tewitfield which was to consist of three inclined planes (similar to that over the Ribble). The line was to ascend 70 feet at Tewitfield, then rise gradually for a further 10 feet to Crooklands, passing east of Lane Hill to Stainton. It was then to use Fletcher's line to the east of Stainton Hill, avoiding the gunpowder works, where it would ascend another 40 feet by an inclined plane to its highest level, then gradually descend 13 feet to Natland. At Natland it was to descend 32 feet by the final inclined plane to Natland Mill and proceed on to Kendal. The tramroad, it was estimated, would cost £38,754; the cheaper canal would cost £71,734.

Wakefield's gunpowder interests at Sedgwick influenced the committee. John Wakefield was a large and influential shareholder in the canal company. He saw the canal as a means of transporting gunpowder. His decision to relocate the gunpowder works to Gatebeck led to the canal being diverted from Rennie's original line to its present route. The

Dovehouses Bridge and Farleton Feeder coming in from the left

canal committee decided to adopt the Hincaster line, the canal to be 27 feet wide at the top and 15 feet at the bottom with a 4 feet 6 inches depth of water. This was endorsed at the General Meeting of 7 January 1805. This line virtually followed Whitworth's original line. On 13 August 1807 their Bill for varying Rennie's line between Tewitfield and Hincaster and building tramroads to Farleton Knott and Kellet Seeds was passed (this also permitted the construction of tramroads within the line of the canal, thus authorising, retrospectively, the building of the Preston tramroad). The stipulation that the canal must be 7 feet deep from Kendal to Hincaster Green, and the provisions for taking water from the River Mint were, however, repealed. Water was to be abstracted from Stainton, Crooklands, and Farleton Becks instead.

A flight of eight locks at Tewitfield was to raise the level by 76 feet. The canal was to pass to the east of Holme, through Farleton and Crooklands to Stainton, where it was to turn west and pass beneath Hincaster Hill in a 378 yard tunnel and then turn north towards Kendal. On 7 February 1809 it was resolved 'That the Committee be directed and authorised to proceed with the execution of that part of the canal between Tewitfield and Kendal.' However, owing to the Napoleonic Wars and a lack of funds, four more years were to elapse before construction started. That meeting also reported that bridges made of timber were mostly in bad condition and would require renewing. Whenever possible, that would be in stone. The February 1810 General Meeting resolved that the canal be extended from its terminus, across the road at Bark Hill, to a new one two or three hundred yards further on. This had been requested as the deep and narrow road prevented convenient access to the canal. It was estimated that the extension would cost £2,459, including building a warehouse. At that meeting it was foreseen that considerable repairs to the timber bridges over the Ribble would be needed and also the rebuilding of some of the swivel bridges.

In 1810, the committee bought 86 acres of land on Killington Common, five miles east of Kendal near the Sedbergh area fells. The land secured was common land which was of little value. This was ready for a reservoir for the Kendal level. The reservoir is now, of course, readily seen from Killington Services on the M6.

1810 also saw the Lancaster committee reaching agreement with the Leeds and Liverpool over their use of part of the South End. The Lancaster was to construct seven locks at Johnson's Hillock, rising 64 feet to join with the Leeds and Liverpool line and a short extension from Bark Hill towards Wigan (which was already under construction). This did not mean that all squabbling ended, and in 1811 a serious dispute arose with twelve Leeds and Liverpool shareholders over alleged favouritism in the placing of contracts. Gregson and several of the committee men were accused of receiving favoured treatment in regard to their private business activities on the canal, and with their coal mining interests. Naturally a committee of investigation had to be appointed to look into these charges. In their report of 7 August 1812 they not only found the accusations to be unfounded, but ended by praising Gregson and several of the committee members for their enterprise in setting up in 1797 as canal carriers to promote trade to the benefit of the Company. In addition they pointed out that Gregson had carried out duties far in excess of his office of clerk, and for no payment. 'To his enterprize on the opening of the Canal, and to his subsequent indefatigable exertions, united with those of the Committee, may be attributed the progressive increase of the Tonnage Duties.' In addition the committee were praised for raising money on their own securities when they could make no further calls on shareholders.

1812 saw the start of further activities for the completion of the 14.5 miles of line to Kendal. Thomas Cartwright was appointed engineer that year and instructed to make detailed estimates of the revenue potential and cost of the line. It was estimated that income would increase by a total of £7,589 per year (including £1,000 for the diversion of coastal trade from Milnthorpe to Lancaster and then on by canal), and £500 would be saved in the expense of pumping water at Preston owing to the amount which the locks would bring down. The cost of the extension was estimated at £98,095. At the end of the year it was resolved to begin work and the contract for making Hincaster Tunnel was let. Shuttleworth, one of the Preston proprietors, and several others put forward a scheme for crossing the Ribble on the level. At the same time as starting the Kendal line, Fletcher was asked to advise on this further scheme which he declared impracticable. Another scheme followed, which this time Fletcher agreed could be done although it would endanger water supplies. It was for a lower level aqueduct, involving more lockage on both sides. As it was estimated that it would cost £160,537, nearly twice the amount for the whole Kendal extension, there were obviously no funds available. At a Special General Meeting held in 1817, on Shuttleworth's demand, his resolution that an application be made for a loan from the Exchequer Bill Loan Commissioners was defeated.

Work was proceeding with both Hincaster Tunnel and Tewitfield Locks, the major engineering tasks of this section, work on the tunnel having been let in 1813. The annual report to the General Meeting on 7 February 1815 reveals the doubts and difficulties the committee had over the lining of the tunnel as, to them, brick was an inferior material to stone.

> The deep Cutting at both ends of Hincaster Tunnel is proceeding and the Excavation of the Tunnel is let. Much difficulty has arisen in endeavouring to procure stone for the Arching of this Tunnel. Limestone being the only stone within many miles of the work, and the quarries not yielding material of necessary dimensions, without very great expense, your Committee have some thoughts of arching the Tunnel with brick. From the opinions they have already taken [note: these investigations were in the Midlands] it does appear that Bricks have been generally used for Tunnels and the oldest Works in the Kingdom are formed with them, they have been found durable and the use greatly facilitates the execution. Within a short distance of the Tunnel [below Moss Side Farm near Heversham in fact], clay may be got – your Committee have procured some, and the bricks which have been made from it have the appearance of good and sound bricks and have met with the approbation of the engineers, who have seen them, and who have been accustomed to similar works. Your Committee are persuing their enquiries and investigations respecting the nature of this clay, and should the result prove satisfactory, much time as well as expense will be saved in the execution on the Tunnel.

It was also reported at that meeting that works on the junction with the Leeds and Liverpool Canal should be completed during the summer, but the junction was not actually opened until 22 October 1816.

At the 1816 General Meeting the committee reported that the aqueduct over Stainton Beck and the Moss Lane Aqueduct were finished, and a considerable quantity of materials were laid down for those over Crooklands and Farleton Becks. The masonry on one of the locks was complete whilst the others were in a state of forwardness. The deep cuttings at each end of Hincaster Tunnel were complete and one length of open cutting at the northern end complete. The southern end was ready for masonry as soon as the season would admit it. The first 10 yards at each end of the tunnel was to be lined with stone and the remainder with bricks, three hundred and fifty thousand of which had been made the previous summer. On 4 February 1817 it was reported that two million bricks had been made and that nearly half the tunnel was complete. On Christmas day the same year the tunnel was completed. Following its completion, Thomas Fletcher sold the remaining ten thousand bricks.

May 1817 saw William Crossley appointed independently of Fletcher to complete the work north of the locks and also the construction of Killington Reservoir. It had been appreciated by the committee that the rivers feeding the canal would be inadequate during the summer months. Land was secured on common land which was of little value.

On 30 June 1817 the construction of the line from Hincaster to Kendal was publicly let. There were several navvies at the meeting and afterwards they caused considerable riot in the town. The *Westmorland Advertiser* of 5 July 1817 claimed that sound policy demanded that the ruffians should be held up as an example to the unruly multitude which the cutting of the canal was to bring to the populous neighbourhood. By the end of 1818 the locks were completed; Fletcher was praised for their plan and the manner in which the workmanship was executed. By 27 March 1819 the canal was filled with water to Crow Park (west of Natland) and by 14 April, the first boat came up to the Aynam Basin.

The accounts to 31 December 1818 showed that to that date the cost of the lockage and completing the canal in Lancashire had been £8,791 5s. 9d. and the works in Westmorland had cost £33,534 19s. 5d.

The official opening should have been held on 1 May 1819, but this was postponed owing to an embankment bursting 7 miles from Kendal. On 18 June the canal was opened with all due ceremony. At 7.00 a.m. the gentlemen of the Kendal Town Corporation, preceded by a band and a party of special constables, processed down the canal basin where they embarked on the Corporation barge, accompanied by a party of ladies. Another barge was filled with gaily attired occupants. All business had been closed in the town, flags had been hoisted and cannon were fired from time to time. At 10.15 a.m. to the ringing of bells, the flotilla set sail to Crooklands where they awaited the Lancaster contingent, which included five trading boats of Messrs Hargreaves, Welch and Company and three packet boats. The full procession of sixteen boats then returned to Kendal, arriving at the basin at 5.00 p.m. It was conjectured that ten thousand people were on the side of Castle Hill awaiting the event. There followed a dinner for one hundred and twenty at the town hall, with the mayor presiding, and a ball in the Assembly Rooms. So, after twenty-seven years in construction, the main line was complete from Preston.

The completion of the canal had an immediate effect on Kendal. Nicholson (in the *Annals of Kendal*, 2nd edition, 1861) says:

the spirit of improvement fully manifested itself in 1818 and 1819. The date of the new town may, we conceive, truly be placed here at the time of the opening of the Lancaster and Kendal Canal. This event gave an impulse to the public spirit of the inhabitants and formed the commencement of a new era in the history of Kendal ... The old Miller's Close Bridge, which had stood since 1743, and was very narrow and ill adapted to the general medium of intercourse with the canal, was now thrown down and wholly rebuilt on a wider scale. The large warehouses and other buildings at the canal harbour, were all erected at this time; Kent Lane (which before was very steep, and so narrow that two carts could scarcely pass) was thrown open and the ascent considerably diminished; Long Pool was widened; Gandy Street erected; Kent Terrace and Castle Crescent were built shortly after. The Union Building Society commenced operations about this time; and indeed on every side, numerous habitations were superadded to the town ... in a very short time the town assumed a new and modern appearance – so very different that any person having been absent for a few years, could scarcely have identified it.

Whilst the building of the canal extension was in progress, in 1818 the Kendal Town Corporation undertook the building of the basin, wharves and warehouses and Miller Bridge at a cost to them of £7,004 11s. 6d. The expected income from the wharves and warehouses was £550 per annum but there were some expenses against this. The Lancaster Canal Company agreed, in return, to take the canal a few yards further on at Aynam.

The grounds where the canal ended were known as 'Tenter Grounds'. Tenters were frames of wood and later of wrought iron, that were fitted with sharp hooks at the top and bottom. Processed woollen cloth was stretched on tenters to dry. There were 680 yards of tenters which had to be moved from Aynam and compensation of £227 was paid.

Killington Reservoir was constructed to feed the canal extension. As has been mentioned, the committee purchased 86 acres of land in 1810 ready for this work. It was completed by the time the Kendal section of the canal was opened. The embankment has been raised several times so that the reservoir now covers 153 acres and has a capacity of 4,000,000 cubic yards. It is one of the largest canal feeders in the country. Water is sent down Crooklands Beck as required, there originally being safeguards for the interests of mill owners on the beck. Not long after the reservoir was filled, a leak was discovered in the dam and the whole had to be drained to make the necessary repair. Much of the embankment had to be taken down to locate the cause of the leak. When this was done, forty cart-loads of fine red trout weighing 6–7 pounds each were caught and taken to Kendal market for sale.

CHAPTER 3

The Stable Years

THE LANCASTER CANAL COMPANY now sought a sixth and final Act of Parliament. The proprietors now wished to build the Glasson Dock branch (which had been authorised in the 1793 Act) in an endeavour to improve the fortunes of the Port of Lancaster and provide a link with the sea. More capital was required and so the Bill was drafted seeking the necessary powers. There was immediate opposition to the Bill, particularly from Preston, where a canal crossing of the Ribble to make a through connection with the coalfields (thus eliminating the cost of carrying coal over the tramroad) was considered more important. In the *Preston Chronicle* it was observed that the Company had wasted enough money in 'ornamenting the town of Lancaster with a grand aqueduct over the Lune, upon which the water had laid stagnant for over twenty years.' The proposal to build a branch to Glasson Dock now in the hopes of reviving 'the decayed port of Lancaster' was seen as an unfair indulgence. Once again, however, Lancaster had its way and the Act of Parliament was obtained on 14 June 1819. Retrospectively it authorised both the building of Killington Reservoir and the connection at Johnson's Hillock with the Leeds and Liverpool, to which the 2s. 3d. Toll under the 1792 Act was to apply. Powers were given to raise a mortgage of £270,000 on the tolls so as to finance the work on the Glasson Dock branch and repay debts.

William Crosley was appointed superintendent of the entire canal in 1820. His estimate of the cost of the Glasson Dock branch was £34,608 and a decision to commence work on it was reached at the February 1823 General Meeting. Before reaching this decision, however, consideration was given to a connection with the sea at Hest Bank, the canal's nearest point to the sea, only a quarter of a mile from the foreshore. There was a stone pier here, built in 1820, and goods were transhipped from coastal vessels (particularly from Liverpool and Glasgow) for forwarding to Kendal by canal, then by road carrier to destinations such as Penrith, Kirkby Stephen and Hawes. In 1820 four vessels sailed from Liverpool every four or five days. Crosley estimated the cost of this linkage, including a dock (behind which was presumably the Hest Bank Shipping

Looking down the Glasson Arm from Bridge 1

Company) at £69,591. At the time the Glasson decision was taken the Company resolved, probably to placate the shippers, that a drawback of 1s. 8d. a ton on merchandise trans-shipped for Kendal at Hest Bank would be allowed. In anticipation of diverting trade from Preston and exporting coal from Glasson, Lancaster Port Commissioners, who were and are the owners of Glasson Dock, agreed to reduce their dues from 1s. 3d. to 4d. per ton for vessels passing through the branch. In return the Company paid the Port Commissioners £500, in two instalments, and guaranteed them a yearly income of £2000 from ships from the Isle of Man, Ireland and beyond Galloway and Holyhead (trade from these areas then being of some size).

In December 1825, Crosley reported that the 2.5 mile Glasson Branch was ready. However the usual cash shortage delayed the construction of warehouses and wharves, leading to slow growth in trade at first. Eventually a five-storey warehouse capable of dealing with 1,500 tons of goods at once was built. The commodious basin, having a depth of fourteen feet and covering 36,000 square yards, could take larger seagoing vessels as well as canal traffic.

The dividend payment for 1826 was raised to 1½ per cent in spite of the failure of Messrs Dilworth, Arthington and Birkett's bank, which lost the Company £4,500. Also as a result of the failure, a new treasurer had to be appointed. In 1828 the dividend was back at 1 per cent again. Under the 1819 Act, mortgages of £134,550 had been raised and interest rates were rising, being 4 per cent in 1825 and 5 per cent in 1826. The Glasson Dock branch was opened on 16 May 1826 with the passage through it of the sloop *Sprightly*, carrying a cargo of slate from the Duddon to Preston. It was August of the following year before the first vessel sailed through to Kendal. This was the 60-ton schooner *Seaforth* with a cargo of salt from Northwich. Both vessels were Preston registered.

In June 1826, the Glasson branch being open, Crosley resigned in order to take up the appointment of engineer to the Macclesfield Canal. He was succeeded by Samuel Gregson's son, Bryan Padgett Gregson, who had been assisting him since 1813 and was by now in charge of the canal's day-to-day management. He was particularly involved in the development of the packet-boat services running on the North End.

By 1823 the Canal Company had spent £600,000 on capital projects, which, of course, does not include the Glasson Branch. However, as recompense, both tonnage and gross income had risen steadily over the years (see below).

Table 1: Increase in Tonnage Carried on the Canal between 1813 and 1825

| | South End and Tramroad | | North End | Whole Canal |
	Coal in Tons	Total Tons	Total Tons	Final Total
1813	90,000	109,000	113,000	222,000
1820	121,000	179,000	115,000	294,000
1825	215,000	303,000	156,000	459,000

The last two years are with the canal now open to Kendal.

Table 2: Income Generated by the Canal 1807–1823

	North End	South End	Packet boats	Interest, Rents etc.	Total
1807	£6,181	£6,111	£818	£522	£13,632
1808	£7,015	£5,758	£300	£558	£13,631
1809	£7,154	£6,651	£478	£457	£14,740
1810	£7,758	£7,615	£602	£749	£16,715
1811	£8,572	£7,657	£793	£704	£17,726
1812	£9,039	£7,842	£445	£1,367	£18,693
1813	£9,501	£9,267	£572	£865	£20,205
1814	£8,913	£9,927	£749	£831	£20,420
1815	£8,264	£8,568	£477	£1,005	£18,314
1816	£8,406	£10,060	£310	£1,096	£19,872
1817	£7,589	£10,225	£184	£1,085	£19,083
1818	£9,268	£12,509	£232	£1,602	£23,611
1819	£11,140	£11,246	0	£1,533	£23,919
1820	£12,803	£12,486	£43	£1,344	£26,676
1821	£11,875	£12,050	£590	£1,404	£25,919
1822	£11,696	£12,417	£630	£1,124	£25,867
1823	£12,870	£14,199	£247	£1,558	£28,874

The rise in income following the opening of the canal through to Kendal in 1819 will be noted. (Source: Baines's Lancashire.)

Glasson trade increased at the expense of Milnthorpe, Preston and Hest Bank, which finished as a port in 1831 when the Hest Bank Company transferred to Glasson. Milnthorpe, and later Sandside, which became the port for Milnthorpe and was once known as Milnthorpe Sandside, declined as the port for Kendal and was finally made redundant in 1857 with the arrival of the Ulverston and Lancaster Railway (the viaduct of which caused silting and changes in the Kent Estuary). The trade to the Lancaster quays remained comparatively stable, as did the town's growth for a time. However the coming of the canal and tramroad ensured that Preston flourished.

In 1804 the population of Preston was about 10,000, but by 1825 it had risen to over 30,000. The opening of the Glasson branch had helped foster the growth of the town, but it did little for the Ribble Navigation Company. The Ribble was difficult to navigate owing to sandbanks, silting and shifting channels. Imported goods were transferred to lighters off Lytham and landed at Preston quay at a cost of 14s. 10d. per ton; the cost of importing to Preston via Glasson and the new canal was only 13s. 9d. per ton and there was no need for smaller craft to trans-ship at Glasson. In 1829 the Ribble Navigation Company stated that 'Scotch and Foreign trade vessel have left the port for the superior advantages of Glasson.' Eventually, in 1838, a new company was formed to take measures to restore trade to the Ribble.

In 1830, 16,306 tons passed through Glasson Dock, the bulk of it continuing on to the canal. In the same year sixty-four ships carrying 4,633 tons passed over the canal from Glasson from the £200 guarantee area. By 1840 these figures had risen to one hundred and eighty-five ships carrying 12,128 tons. (In addition there must have been other ships from within the guarantee area which sailed up the canal, but these cannot be identified with certainty.) Trade outwards was coal to North Wales, Ireland and Ulverston; inwards it was mainly slate, timber, grain and potatoes.

1827 saw another scheme published by Twyford and Wilson, civil engineers and surveyors from Manchester. It was the last proposal, until the Millennium Ribble Link, to unite the Lancaster with the Leeds and Liverpool canals via the Douglas. Their Ribble crossing was to be by wooden booms moored across the river from the mouth of the Douglas to Freckleton, forming a floating towpath. Two navigation channels were to be left in the middle; on the crossing of these the authors were significantly silent! A new canal from Freckleton was to rise by 79 feet 4 inches via ten locks and join the Lancaster near Salwick. From it, another canal would be made crossing the Fylde to Thornton via Kirkham and

Poulton-le-Fylde. A harbour was proposed at Thornton, further up the Wyre than Fleetwood which became a port in its own right twenty-two years later, having originally been opened under Preston in 1840. This scheme would have seen the end of the hindrance of the Lancaster's tramroad and brought trade from cargoes of grain to be carried from the Fylde. It was estimated that 11.25 miles of new canal would cost under £80,000. Neither the Lancaster nor the Leeds and Liverpool took any interest in the scheme.

By this time the shadow which was to be cast over the Lancaster Canal and others, and which would eventually lead to their demise as commercial waterways, was already on its way – the railway era was about to begin.

CHAPTER 4

The Coming of the Railways

I N 1831 WIGAN AND PRESTON RAILWAY was authorised, a line running roughly parallel to the canal but some distance away. In a report dated 20 July 1830, during the promotion of the line, B. P. Gregson put forward four alternative suggestions to meet this danger to the canal. The first was the conversion of the tramroad into a railway in order to speed the trans-shipment of goods. The second was the same, but with suitable deviations to permit its being worked by locomotive. The third was the possibility of amalgamation with the railway and the abolition of the tramroad. The final alternative was to abolish the tramroad, leaving the South End for the sole use of the Leeds and Liverpool and so forcing the railway to make branches to the pits on the canal. Gregson realised that railways were here to stay and pointed out that if the Canal Company opposed the Wigan and Preston Railway, another scheme would soon take its place. The pattern of trade was bound to change and the Company should accept the fact. Gregson felt that if the committee were to insist on opposing the railway, the most effective method of doing so would be to promote one of its own instead.

The committee decided to look into the first alternative and appointed George Stephenson to investigate the possibility of the tramroad conversion. His recommendation was for two diversions and four self-acting inclines, the existing engine-worked incline from the bridge over the Ribble being retained. In his report to the committee Gregson said, 'I cannot but consider Mr Stephenson's plan attended with many difficulties and inconveniences, not only in execution, but even in operation.' The cost of the plan was estimated to be £11,895.

These were the days of railway mania and more lines were being promoted – for example, Manchester to Bolton and Bolton to Preston via Chorley were two such, of consequence to the canal. Where it was advantageous, the Lancaster's policy was to compete, otherwise it co-operated. In 1834 the North Union Railway, of which the Wigan and Preston had become a part, opened its main line through to Preston and also a branch line from Wigan to New Springs. The branch crossed the line, authorised

Site of Garstang and Knott End Railway

by Parliament, of the Lancaster Canal to West Houghton. It did so at a point just beyond the junction with the Leeds and Liverpool Canal at Wigan Top Lock. As a result, in 1836 the Lancaster Canal Company hastily extended their line a few hundred yards towards Westhoughton so as to force the railway to build a bridge. Since the Company had abandoned all hopes of completing their line by then, this extension was useless. Its purpose was to make the North Union Railway, who had refused agreement to a protective clause being included in their Bill, realise they could not ride roughshod over the canal.

The Bolton and Preston Railway's line, however, followed the canal so closely that the Company was forced to reach an agreement with them. The railway company also wanted to use the tramroad route to gain entry to Preston. An agreement was reached in January 1837 whereby the tramroad was leased to the railway in perpetuity, together with land for a station to be built near the Preston basin. The railway was to receive all tolls from the South End traffic other than those from the Leeds and Liverpool. In exchange the railway's promoter agreed to pay the Company a rent of £8,000 per annum and construct a short transfer siding from their Preston terminus to the canal basin. A locomotive was to be reserved exclusively to operate the transferred traffic between the Canal Company's North End and South End. In July 1837 the railway company obtained its Act, and a year later obtained a second one which authorised the company to enter Preston over the North Union's metals from Euston, thus leaving them saddled with a tramroad which was no longer required. Not surprisingly the Lancaster Canal Company had no desire to take it back. Eventually the railway company agreed to maintain the tramroad for the Canal Company's use at a reduced rental of £7,400, thus allowing for the expense of the upkeep. Later the rental was reduced to £7,000 by the Company itself, rather than allow the benefit of preferential coal rates go to the railway company for traffic transferred at Preston to the North End.

Gregson foresaw that the railways would build branches to the collieries and gradually take over the canal's coal traffic, so he therefore advised disposing of the tramroad when the opportunity arose. In 1865 he explained that 'The result otherwise would have been the loss of nearly the whole of that Traffic and a considerable outlay in repairs. This agreement also secured and improved the Coal Traffic of the North End by connection with the North Union and the Bolton and Preston Railway at Preston.' By concentrating on the North End, with its long established trade, through the newly built transfer sidings at Preston, the Company gained cheap supplies of coal which they were able to export through Glasson.

Meanwhile, other events were taking place. 1836 saw the Ribble pumping engine and land sold because Killington Reservoir had proved itself adequate in supplying the canal. Following two collapses in 1827, with a third in 1836, the Whittle Hill Tunnel was opened out in the middle in 1838 in order to form two separate short tunnels.

In 1837 a Bill proposing the inevitable railway to Lancaster, the Lancaster and Preston Junction Railway, was put before Parliament. The Company objected to the Bill as the proposed line crossing 'the Canal Company's Wharfs, west of the Canal in Preston, will deprive them of convenience and facilities, absolutely necessary in the formation of a Basin, Coal Yard and Wharfs.' They wished a clause to be inserted in the Act to prevent the railway company from entering upon any of their land or property without their consent. The eventual outcome was that some land at Dock Street was sold to the railway company.

The construction of a ship canal from Lytham Pool to Marsh Lane in Preston had been proposed in the 1830s. As this would have been separate from the Lancaster by only 600 yards, there had been talk of connecting the two. Nothing came of the scheme. During this time of change and uncertainty, trade had still continued to grow, reaching the peak year for the whole canal in 1840 (see below).

The year 1837 saw the dividend rising to 1.25 per cent whilst in 1840 it was 1.35 per cent. Repayment of mortgages was also continuing steadily. However, June 1840 saw the opening of the railway to Lancaster, an event that was to have unusual repercussions on the future of the Lancaster Canal.

Table 3: Increase in Tonnage and Revenue on the Canal between 1836 and 1840.

| | South End & Tramroad | | North End | | |
	Coal in Tons	Total Tons	Total Tons	Final Total	Revenue
1836	251,000	377,000	173,000	550,000	£33,000
1840	291,000	424,000	193,000	617,000	£34,200

CHAPTER 5

The Lancaster and Preston Junction Railway

IT IS USEFUL AT THIS POINT to turn to the history of the Lancaster and Preston Junction Railway, which came to be the Lancaster Canal's major competitor.

The Lancaster and Preston Junction Railway, which opened on 25 June 1840, had an end-on junction with the North Union at Preston. The two had a joint working agreement to this and shared the station, although agreement to this had been reached with difficulty. Three weeks later the Preston and Wyre Railway, which also had the use of the North Union station, was opened to Fleetwood. It became a competitor of the Lancaster and Preston Junction for Scottish traffic when a steamer service to Ardrossan opened in May 1841.

The Lancaster Canal Company halved their fares (see Chapter Nine) between Lancaster and Preston on the opening of the railway, and continued to carry roughly the same number of passengers as before, probably helped by several minor accidents on the railway which caused delays to traffic. In June 1841 the North Union gave the Lancaster and Preston notice of termination of their joint working agreement on 31 December. Agreement was reached with the Bolton and Preston Railway that their Preston station would be completed and that the Lancaster and Preston would have use of it from 1 January 1842. The North Union then protested that the termination of the agreement was not intended to cover the use of their station, and a bitter quarrel between the companies developed over this which resulted in inconvenience to passengers, some of whom used the canal instead.

The opening of the Bolton and Preston line was delayed owing to construction difficulties at the tunnel and cuttings near Chorley, and this meant less traffic than anticipated for the Lancaster and Preston Junction. Also, rather than carrying on to Lancaster, it had become more convenient to use the Preston Wharf to transfer northern traffic to the Canal directly. As a result of all this, takings fell short of expectations and the railway company found itself in financial difficulties. The Lancaster and Preston Junction Railway, panic stricken, sought a purchaser, but their terms were not acceptable to either its friend the Bolton and Preston, or to the North Union. They next sought a deal with the Lancaster Canal Company, who seized their chance and reversed the more usual procedure of railways purchasing canals. The meeting agreeing to the transfer of the Lancaster and Preston Junction Railway Company to the Canal Company took place in the Directors' Room at its Penny Street or Greaves Station on 10 August 1842. The meeting had started half an hour late to allow for anyone arriving on the 12.30 train.

The 1843 General Meeting of the Canal Company was told that the Committee had done this with a view to the protection of the revenue of the canal. However, they also appreciated that there was a threat from the proposed extension of the railway from Lancaster to Carlisle. On 1 September 1842 they took a twenty-one year lease on the Lancaster and Preston Junction Railway.

The Company was to pay a rent of £13,300 per annum (which represented a 4 per cent dividend) and take on the interest payments on the £113,300 which had been borrowed by the railway company. Moreover, the Company undertook not to oppose the projected railway to Carlisle and if the line was completed within the twenty-one years, to agree to an increase in the rental. An Act of Parliament empowering the lease was passed on 3 April 1843. At that time there were two schemes mooted for lines between Lancaster and Carlisle; one for a line via Kirkby Lonsdale that went up the Lune Valley, the other for a line via Kendal. Naturally the Lancaster Canal Company favoured the former as it would not be in direct competition with them, and they even promised to invest £50,000 in the scheme. However, they were forced to withdraw their offer so as to put off opposition to the railway company's leasing bill.

The Manchester, Bolton and Bury had worked the Lancaster and Preston Junction line by earlier agreement. On the Lancaster Canal Company's acquisition of that railway's locomotives, the arrangement was continued by a new agreement which also provided for the engines to work to Bolton. The North Union had wished to enter a joint agreement for the Preston–Manchester traffic, an offer which was rejected and which resulted in bitter competition between them and the Bolton and Preston until the amalgamation of the two companies on 1 January 1844. This amalgamation forced the Lancaster Canal Company to reach an agreement with the North Union and it started using their station again from 12 February 1844.

By this time the Lancaster and Carlisle Railway plans had taken shape, the route via Kendal having been chosen. The new railway company quickly reached a provisional agreement with the Company whereby the latter would manage the North End and the Glasson branch for and on behalf of the railway company for a guaranteed income of £11,000 per annum. As the canal's receipts for the second half of 1843 totalled £10,223, the Company evidently anticipated that there would be a considerable fall in revenue on the opening of the railway. The Company offered the Lancaster and Carlisle Railway an option on the remaining years of the lease of the Lancaster and Preston Junction at £1,250 per annum, stone from the Company's quarry at Lancaster for use in constructing the line and general assistance in building the railway. However, as usual, disagreement arose, this time over the inclusion in the agreement of the wharves at Preston. The Company therefore opposed the Lancaster and Carlisle's Bill, but in June 1844 the railway was authorised.

By this time reasons had been found for believing that the lease of the Lancaster and Preston Junction Railway to the Lancaster Canal Company was illegal. The Act of 1843 only gave powers for the lease and did not refer to the terms which had been agreed upon. The draft of the lease, although it was supposed to have taken effect from 1 September 1842, was not presented to the railway company until 1843 when it was found to contain clauses permitting a sub-lease. No doubt this was to permit sub-leasing of the railway to the Lancaster and Carlisle, which had now been approved. The railway company objected to this, as they too were interested in leasing their line to the new Lancaster and Carlisle Railway. Subsequent negotiations with the Lancaster Canal Company were unsuccessful so that in October 1844 the two railway companies considered themselves free to come to terms by themselves. The Lancaster and Preston was leased to the Lancaster and Carlisle from 1 September 1846.

Before continuing with the saga of the Lancaster and Preston Junction Railway, other events in the life of the Lancaster Canal should be brought up to date. The Canal Company worked the railway very successfully from their own point of view, but not in the eyes of its users. Their first act on acquiring the railway had been to withdraw the packet boats between Preston and Lancaster, at the same time increasing the fares by train and removing the seats from the third class coaches to make room for more passengers. A letter from 'Not a Well-wisher to Tub-travelling, but to the Public at Large', appeared in the *Lancaster Guardian* in 1843, complained at having to pay 2s. 6d. to travel to Preston and only be able to sit on the floor with a good chance of being trodden on! When the trains stopped, he complained, all the passengers were jostled together. Another complaint against the Canal Company during that period was that, on one train, second class passengers not travelling through to London and were also conveyed in a third class carriage.

The General Meeting on 7 February 1843 reported that the general depression of trade had continued and that four weeks of frost in January 1842 also caused trade to be considerably less than in the previous year. Even so, the Committee still recommended that a dividend of one pound ten shillings (£1.50) should be paid.

In 1845 Hargreaves and Son ceased carrying merchandise on the railway, leaving the Lancaster Canal Company with an absolute monopoly of all passenger and freight traffic over both railway and canal. This they exploited, making a profit of £5,000 from the railway in 1845 which was then considerably increased in each of the following years. Strange to relate, most of the blame from the public for the way the railway was run was laid at the Lancaster and Preston Junction's door, not the Canal Company's.

Glasson Dock continued to thrive until 1846, when trade started to fall. There was by now a challenge from Fleetwood (to where the Preston and Wyre Railway line had been opened) and, with ships growing in size, the difficulties of entering Glasson increased because of the sandbanks in the Lune Estuary. Improvements on the Ribble posed a further threat to Glasson. As has been mentioned, a new company was incorporated in 1838 to cut a new and deeper channel up the river, to enlarge the quay at Preston and build a dock at Lytham where large ships unable to pass up the river could discharge their cargoes into lighters. This scheme was completed in 1842, and a branch railway opened in 1846.

To combat this, three new schemes were put forward in Lancaster in the 1840s. One was Stephenson's scheme to improve the river by deepening the channel to the Lancaster quays. Another scheme was for the construction of a new dock at Thornbush (which had been the site of a canal scheme in 1799) with a railway to the Lancaster and Preston Junction line at Ellel. The third, and most seriously considered scheme was for docks to be constructed at Poulton Ring (now Morecambe), these being connected to the Lune at Lancaster by a ship canal 3.5 miles in length across the peninsula to the river where a dam would maintain deep water at the quays.

Edmund Sharpe, a Poulton landowner who was also an engineer and architect, proposed this scheme. He was the secretary of the 'little' North Western Railway whose line from Skipton was originally planned to terminate at Lancaster. The intention was that an improved port at Lancaster would further trade between the West Riding of Yorkshire and the west coast. Capital was available for financing one of the schemes because in order to secure Admiralty consent to bridge the Lune, the Lancaster and Carlisle had paid £16,000 compensation to Lancaster merchants and £10,000 for improvements to the river. When in 1845 the Tidal Harbours Commission held an enquiry into the best method of utilising the £10,000, Sharpe attacked the Thornbush scheme as being yet another blow to the Port of Lancaster from the Lancaster Canal Company who already monopolised the town's communications through being the lessees of the Lancaster and Preston Junction Railway. On behalf of the 'little' North Western Railway, backed by the Midland Railway, Lancaster merchants and Poulton landowners (including Sharpe) went on to press for the ship canal scheme. Both the Lancaster Canal and the Lancaster and Carlisle Railway opposed it as they considered that it would be severely prejudicial to the future of Glasson Dock.

The Morecambe Bay Harbour Company was floated shortly afterwards with a view to building a harbour and making a ship canal to Lancaster. When their formal prospectus came out in November 1845 it was found that a railway had been substituted for a canal, which had been reluctantly given up owing to the anticipated cost of construction. It was estimated that a canal would have cost £50,000 more than had originally been anticipated and, as they were giving the £10,000 for the improvements to the Lune, their opposition would carry weight in Parliament. Whilst there was some agitation from Lancaster for a canal, it was short-lived and, in 1846, the Morecambe Harbour Railway Act was passed having received but little opposition. Later in the year the company was purchased by the 'little' North Western, exercising their option to do so. With the £10,000 from the Lancaster and Carlisle Railway the Lune was deepened, but this was only a temporary improvement and gradually the port at Morecambe took most of the trade. The Midland Railway, who had in turn taken over the 'little' North Western, transferred its shipping activities to the new port at Heysham in 1904.

Discussions between the Lancaster and Carlisle Railway and Lancaster and Preston Junction Railway Companies had continued and, by the end of 1845, the two boards had agreed that an amalgamation should take place immediately. The threat from the 'little' North Western Railway had helped precipitate this as their line from Skipton (where they had a junction with the Midland Railway) to Lancaster and Morecambe was considered by the Lancaster and Preston Junction to be a threat to their own line. Agreement had been reached with the Canal Company allowing it to pass under the Lune Aqueduct. The 'little' North Western Railway was incorporated in 1846.

Barton and Broughton Station. Photograph courtesy of Ben Brooksbank, geograph.org.uk

In February 1846 an Extraordinary General Meeting was held and the directors of the Lancaster and Preston Junction put their proposals to the shareholders for ratification. However, the shareholders felt that better terms could be obtained by waiting until the Lancaster and Carlisle had been built and the Preston–Lancaster traffic had increased. An amendment to the effect that the proposed merger be not carried out received the unanimous support of the shareholders. All but one of the directors (he was not present at the meeting) thereupon resigned. The meeting had no power to appoint a new board as, under their Act, they could only elect three new shareholders to the board at the annual general meeting each June: the quorum was five directors, thus it would be two years before a board would be able to hold a meeting once again.

The railway was now theoretically legally leased to the Lancaster and Carlisle, but in practice it was illegally leased to the Lancaster Canal Company. The Lancaster and Carlisle demanded that the Company surrender the line on 1 July 1846, but they refused to do so, continued running trains as before and started Chancery proceedings against the Lancaster and Preston Junction, seeking an injunction for the enforcement of the lease of 1842.

The Lancaster and Carlisle Railway was opened between Lancaster and Kendal on 22 September 1846. Cheekily, they ran six trains a day through to Preston over the Lancaster and Preston Junction's metals (to which they had constructed a link from their Lancaster Castle Station despite opposition from the Company), without authority and in the face of great protests. The Company also ran local trains between the two towns and on the opening of the line to Kendal, promptly withdrew their Lancaster–Kendal packet-boat services.

The Lancaster and Carlisle Railway added insult to injury by sending statements of their traffic over the Lancaster and Preston Junction line but refusing to pay tolls, claiming that they considered there was no legally constituted body to which they could be paid!

However, the Canal Company had another trick up its sleeve. February 1847 saw the East Lancashire Railway offering to buy both the canal and the Lancaster and Preston Junction Railway. £29,000 outright was to be offered for the railway and the canal was to be purchased for £23,500 per annum, this being redeemable within ten years at twenty-five years' purchase. Agreement was almost reached, but both parties withdrew after the shareholders of the Lancaster and Preston Junction appointed a new, illegal, board of directors to consider the proposal. Then once again the Canal Company tried to enforce the 1842 lease granted by the 1843 Act, but this was summarily dismissed by the railway shareholders who proceeded with their own arrangements for the leasing of the line. The Lancaster and Preston Junction shareholders held a General Meeting on 4 November 1847 when they unanimously rescinded their 1843 agreement to the lease. Committees were then appointed by both the Railway and Canal companies to meet and have discussions on the situation. The Lancaster and Preston junction was determined not to lease to the canal; the Lancaster Canal Company said that it was prepared to dispose of its interest in the railway on payment of adequate compensation. At this time the Company also required support in the execution of their 1844 lease and recovery of tolls from the Lancaster and Carlisle Railway. The Lancaster and Preston Junction refused to lend its support and, in retaliation, the Canal Company withheld its half-yearly rent payment due on 1 March 1848. Each then took legal proceedings against the other to enforce what they considered to be their legal rights.

The Lancaster Canal Company, who in spite of the dispute over tolls were still on comparatively friendly terms with the Lancaster and Carlisle, then turned to that railway company with their rent proposals. They would sell the canal to the railway company outright together with the Lancaster and Preston Junction Railway for 38s. per share plus 5 per cent per annum in perpetuity on payment of outstanding tolls, the amount of which was still being negotiated. The Lancaster and Carlisle then counter-offered 30s. per share, subject to their taking over the Company's suit in Chancery against the Lancaster and Preston Junction and successfully obtaining it. This offer was accepted by the Canal Company, but fell through later due to the Lancaster and Carlisle's desire to make unacceptable changes.

On 21 August 1848 the farce of two companies each running its own trains over the line ended in inevitable tragedy. On that day the 9.00 a.m. Euston to Glasgow express was running one hour fifteen minutes late when, hauled by 'Dalemain', a Lancaster and Carlisle engine, it rounded the curve at Bay Horse. Ahead, too late to pull up, the driver Richard Morris saw a Lancaster and Preston train still standing at Bay Horse station; he ran into its rear, fatally injuring a passenger.

An enquiry under Captain Laffan R.E. of the Board of Trade followed. He found that the signalling on the line was bad, one small red flag on a staff at each station. Among the other causes of the crash he found 'The uncertainty as to who is the rightful possessor of the line' and 'The want of a proper understanding between the Lancaster and Carlisle and the Lessees of the Lancaster and Preston Junction Railway.' Captain Laffan also suggested that the two companies 'should come to a good understanding and that every effort should be made to determine the right ownership of this railway.'

The Railway Commissioners instructed the Lancaster and Preston to set their house in order. October 1848 saw a committee of directors appointed to reach agreement with the Lancaster Canal Company. Agreement was reached on 13 November 1848 and ratified in December 1848 by a special meeting of the canal proprietors. The Company was to be paid £4,875 per annum for the unexpired portion of the twenty-one year lease, with an option to consolidate the full sum plus 5 per cent within the first eighteen months, or 4.5 per cent thereafter during the fifteen year term. The injunction proceedings instigated by the Company were to be withdrawn, each side paying its own costs. The Lancaster and Preston Junction was to promote a Bill seeking parliamentary sanction for itself. If the Bill failed, they agreed that they would ratify the 1842 lease to the Lancaster Canal Company. The Act passed in 1849 went further. Independent agreement had been reached between the Lancaster and Preston Junction and the Lancaster and Carlisle that the former be joined with the latter on a profit-sharing basis. The Lancaster Canal Company had to give up possession of the Lancaster to Preston line from the passing of the Act, and it did so on 1 August 1849. The Lancaster and Carlisle was ordered to pay to the Canal Company the outstanding tolls, the terms to be settled by arbitration. Robert Stephenson was the appointed arbitrator and he awarded the canal £55,551 10s. 7½d., this allowing for working expenses of £22,062 8s. 8d., covering the period to 31 May 1849. A dispute with the Lancaster and Carlisle then arose over the months of June and July and they had to be settled by Mr Stephenson at £6,019 11s. 0d.

Overall, the Lancaster Canal Company came out of the seven years' wrangle very well. They had a profit of £67,391 which enabled them not only to pay off their outstanding mortgages of £26,000, but also to give a £1 17s. 6d. per share bonus to each proprietor and set up a £6,700 contingencies fund.

Compared with other canals, the Lancaster's dividends were consistently low, being 2 per cent in 1845, 2½ per cent in 1846, 2¼ per cent in 1847 and 1848 and then dropping back again to 2 per cent in 1849 and 1850. Glasson trade continued at a fairly steady level from the £200 guarantee area, being £227 15s. 1d. in 1846, £219 10s. 0d. in 1847, £282 8s. 9d. in 1848, £249 18s. 0d. in 1849 and £281 13s. 4d. in 1850. However, the number of vessels over the arm was falling, being only twenty-three from the £200 guarantee area.

Matters would have been much worse if the canal had still been running the tramroad. From 1840 traffic over it declined, partly owing to the Bolton and Preston increasing the tolls. In 1839 there was a net profit of about £1,000 from the South End tolls and tramroad. This was after paying for rent, heavy repairs and maintenance from a gross income of £10,000. By 1850 the North Union Railway, who had acquired the Bolton and Preston, were showing a loss of about £5,600, having received a revenue of only £1,700.

The Lancaster Canal Company fixed B. P. Gregson's salary at a minimum of £1,000 per annum for the rest of his service in recognition of his negotiations with the railway company on their behalf in 1844. In 1846 he accepted the management of the Edinburgh and Glasgow Railway whilst continuing to work for the Canal Company at his full salary. Both employers were agreeable to his dual role. In October 1846 his father, Samuel Gregson, died at the age of eighty-three, after fifty-four years' service. He had assumed duties far beyond those for which the Company paid him in an endeavour to promote its prosperity. In their February 1847 report to the General Meeting, the Committee said that he had retained to the last a lively interest in all that concerned the canal. He was highly respected in Lancaster, where he was twice made mayor. On Samuel's death, B. P. Gregson succeeded him in the appointment of clerk.

In 1850 a traffic sharing agreement was reached between the Lancaster and Carlisle Railway and the Lancaster Canal Company whereby the former carried the passenger and merchandise traffic to Kendal, and the latter retained the coal and heavy goods traffic as well as the traffic between Glasson Dock, Preston and elsewhere. (For destinations beyond Kendal, coal rates were subject to negotiations.) The reaching of this agreement reveals that the Lancaster Canal Company was still a powerful force in north Lancashire although, by this time, railway companies had taken control of the other canals.

CHAPTER 6

The Last Years of the
Lancaster Canal Company

IN 1845 THE LANCASTER CANAL COMPANY offered to 'sell' the South End outright to either the Lancaster and Carlisle Railway or to the Leeds and Liverpool Canal. Subsequently an offer was made to the Leeds and Liverpool alone at a price of £7,000 per annum for the first three years and £6,300 per annum thereafter. (Included in the offer were the locks at Johnson's Hillock and the Anglezarke land.) Not surprisingly, the Leeds and Liverpool declined this offer, but in 1850 they leased all the merchandise tolls of the South End for £4,335 per annum for a twenty-one year term. They had to do this to counter a lawsuit by the Lancaster Canal Company, and the agreement was ratified at a Special General Meeting of the Lancaster Canal Company in October 1851.

Around this time there were abortive negotiations with the Kendal and Windermere Railway for a tramroad from the canal head to the proposed Kendal station. 1851 saw a proposal for another tramroad, which was to expand the canal's traffic, connecting Kendal to Staveley, Birthwaite (now Windermere) and other parts of the Lake District. Nothing came of the scheme and this meant that coal still had to be carted between the canal head and Kendal railway station.

Competition from the Lancaster and Carlisle was by now having an effect on the Glasson trade. In an effort to counter this, long term contracts were entered into for the carriage of coal at reduced rates and, in February 1851, the Company resolved to engage in coastal traffic. Eight vessels, not all in use at the same time, are supposed to have been owned by the Company, but the entries of ships at Glasson show only five. The first vessel to be purchased was the schooner *Woodbine*, which was followed by the *Richard* in 1852. The *Richard* was shortly lost in the Duddon. Next the *Oriental* was purchased and then, in 1853, the *Bloomer* and three more were ordered in 1855. Also in 1855 a screw steamer, the *Dandy*, was tried on the canal. Coal trade with Ireland had grown to such an extent that the Company rented a quay at Belfast and appointed an agent there. However, the boost to the Glasson Revenue was only temporary and the gradual decline, which had started in 1850, continued. Figures in the £200 column of the Lancaster Port Commissioners' Registers show £281 13s. 4d. for 1850, £253 10s. 5d. for 1851, £181 5s. 4d. for 1852, £181 14s. 4d. for 1853, £225 3s. 4d. for 1854, £141 9s. 3d. for 1855, £201 9s. 8d. for 1856 and £194 0s. 8d. for 1857. In 1856 the four vessels' voyages at Glasson totalled 4,732 tons. Even though the returns had dropped below £200, the Port Commissioners never received the difference to make up the £200 guarantee.

In 1853, the Canal Company was reported to the Lancaster and Carlisle for importing pig iron and treacle from Greenock and Glasgow through Glasson to Preston for Blackburn and east Lancashire. These goods were carried at very low rates so as to compete with transport by sea to Fleetwood and Preston. It was felt that the carriage of these goods could be a contravention of the agreement with the railway company and so the Canal Company opened their books for the Lancaster and Carlisle's inspection. The latter raised no objection, even though the report of the jointly appointed referee stated that technically there could have been an infringement. 1856 saw the books inspected again without dispute. However, in September 1858 the Lancaster and Carlisle served notice of its intention to terminate the competition agreement owing to the canal's violation through their carriage of treacle and pig iron. Incidentally, the treacle and iron trade seems to have disappeared after 1860, presumably taken over by the railway.

In May 1856 the Lancaster and Carlisle had leased the short line of the Kendal and Windermere Railway. Upon its acquisition they started to impede the Canal Company's coal supply to the Lake District, encouraging transport to Windermere by rail instead. With old agreements thus disregarded, the Canal Company started new negotiations, but these were broken off by the Lancaster and Carlisle who refused to come to terms whilst the canal continued with the Glasgow traffic in treacle and iron.

By this time, as a result of amalgamations, the London and North Western Railway controlled all the West Coast route to the south of Preston and had an interest in the Lancaster and Carlisle, whose line they had helped to finance and whose board included seven of their own directors. The London and North Western were noted for their lack of friendly co-operation with rivals, canals in particular, and in 1857 they leased the Lancaster and Carlisle outright.

As a result of this change in ownership, the Lancaster Canal Company had to turn elsewhere to acquire traffic. July 1959 saw the steamer *Duchess*, the Lancaster Steam Navigation Company's vessel, begin twice-weekly sailings carrying merchandise between Glasson and Liverpool at a hire charge of £37 10s. 0d. per trip. Steam tugs were tried on the canal and in June 1860 the company purchased two second-hand ones to join the specially built existing one which was already at work. However, the coasting vessels were steadily being lost at sea until, in 1861, the *Woodbine* was the only one left. Trade continued to be poor, the dividend remained constant at 1.75 per cent from 1851 until 1862 when it dropped to £1 13s. 6d, then £1 12s. 0d. in the following year.

In September 1860 the first moves to sell out to the London and North Western Railway seem to have been made. Negotiations proceeded for over two years before terms were agreed and a Bill was promoted in 1863. It successfully passed through the Commons, but the Lancashire and Yorkshire Railway opposed its passage through the Lords because it had a part interest in the tramroad (owing to their being joint lessees of the North Union with the London and North Western) and wished to participate in the lease of the canal. The London and North Western objected to this and withdrew their Bill, but reintroduced it in the next session. Passage was successful and on 29 July 1864 the Bill received Royal Assent. Under the Lancaster Canal Transfer Act the London and North Western Railway was authorised to lease the North End in perpetuity for £12,665 17s. 6d. per annum, whilst the Leeds and Liverpool Canal Company was authorised to lease the South End for £7,075 from 1 July. The canal had never to be closed to navigation. There were to be increased maximum tolls on both ends. Land was allocated at Preston to enlarge the joint station. The London and North Western, with the consent of the Lancashire and Yorkshire Railway, was authorised to close the tramroad between Preston and Bamber Bridge and dispose of its site. Tram wagons had ceased to run in 1859 and for several years before that the line had been virtually disused; in 1868 the chimney and engine house on Avenham Brow were demolished. The section from Bamber Bridge to Walton Summit was retained as there was still sufficient traffic to justify it, this was mainly coal for mills. Under a London and North Western Act of 1879 this section too was finally closed, traffic on it having entirely ceased by then.

At the next general meeting following the leasing of the canal, held in February 1865, the proprietors had to decide what should be done about Gregson, the Secretary of the Company. He presented a lengthy statement setting out the history of the canal during his service and his achievements on its behalf and, in conclusion, thanked the committee for their support during that time. It was at first proposed that he should be paid off with £4,500, but this proposal was hastily withdrawn by the chairman. It was then resolved to keep Gregson on at a salary of £1,000 per annum, which was done until his death on 3 December 1872. He had given sixty years' service to the Company.

The rental now being received from the lease permitted a regular dividend of 1.75 per cent to be paid again and the company invested the £18,293 balance in hand. 1885 saw the final curtain fall on the Lancaster Canal Company when the London and North Western Railway offered to buy the canal outright, to be paid in 4 per cent debenture stock equal to the rental payable under the lease of both ends of the canal. Based on the then prevailing prices this was equivalent to £43 15s. 0d. for each canal share. The proprietors agreed to the terms and the canal was duly invested in the railway company from 1 July 1885 under an Act of 16 July the same year. The South End continued to be leased to the Leeds and Liverpool, the rent being paid to the railway. A final dividend of 1.75 per cent was paid after which the Lancaster Canal Company was formally dissolved on 1 January 1886. A bonus of 10s. 9d. was paid to each proprietor at the last general meeting, leaving a balance of £101 4s. 10d. which was handed to the chairman. As a memento he had a number of commemorative silver medallions showing the Lune Aqueduct struck. And so ended the Lancaster Canal Company after a life of nearly ninety-five years.

CHAPTER 7

Later Events

THE WINDING-UP OF THE LANCASTER CANAL COMPANY was not the end of life for the canal. Much traffic continued to be carried; in 1824 the committee had sold some land to Kendal Gas Company, thus ensuring regular coal traffic from Preston until the coming of the motor lorry (since there was no access by rail to the gas works). In addition there was coal to be carried to the canal-side mills in Lancaster, and other merchandise such as grain, minerals, manure, timber and chemicals from Glasson to go to Wakefield's gunpowder mills. These mills were by now sited at Gatebeck, further up Crooklands Beck, having replaced the old mills at Sedgwick and Bassingill in 1850. In 1874 the mills were connected by a horse tramway to the canal at Crooklands wharf. However, as the tramway continued beside the main road to Milnthorpe where it connected with the railway, it is probable that the canal only carried a relatively small portion of the traffic during the later years.

The London and North Western Railway managed the canal from Lancaster Castle station where a superintendent was based. In 1883 they opened a branch line from that station to Glasson Dock. Even so, in 1894 the Glasson–Kendal route was still the cheapest for heavy goods such as cement for Thirlmere waterworks, although by this time the grain trade was dwindling rapidly.

Table 4: Decrease in Tonnage and Income from the Canal as shown by the three sample years of 1888, 1890 and 1905.

Year	Tonnage	Tolls	Net Income
1888	173,882	£9,181	£17,289
1890	165,005	£8,013	£18,728
1905	130,396	£6,171	£13,984

Apart from a steam ice-breaker, dredger, two Leeds and Liverpool steam tugs and those mentioned in the last chapter, horse haulage was always used on the canal during its commercial life. The steam tugs were tried for a short period after World War I, but owing to the shallow depth of the canal they could not be fully loaded and so were returned to the Leeds and Liverpool. A new craft used on the canal during its later years came and went by sea between Farleton and Glasson.

In 1923 the London and North Western Railway, and therefore the canal also became part of the London, Midland and Scottish Railway (LMS). By an Act of 1935 the LMS received powers to raise tolls and was authorised to close half a mile of the canal at Kendal owing to leakages from its bed, this being done in 1939. Around 1941 or 1942 the canal north of Kendal gasworks was closed. In 1944 the LMS promoted a Bill seeking to close a number of their canals, including the Lancaster. Owing to opposition from several Lancaster firms and from local authorities, all reference to the Lancaster was deleted in the Lords Committee stage. At that time between 6,500 and 7,500 tons of coal a year were being taken by canal to Kendal gasworks since there was no railway access. However, in September 1944 this traffic was transferred to road on the cessation of all commercial traffic north of Lancaster. In 1947 the last goods were carried from Preston to Lancaster, this being a load of coal for Storey's White Cross Mill by Penny Street Bridge at Lancaster.

Upon the nationalisation of the railways in 1948, the British Transport Commission acquired the Lancaster Canal. Under the transport Act, 1955, they were authorised to close it to navigation and, owing to leakage through limestone fissures in its bed (a problem since Crossley's days), the 5.75 miles north of Stainton Crossing Bridge were drained. The last two miles from Natland into Kendal were filled in.

At the Preston end the basins were still in use to around 1960, but the warehouse had been demolished as far back as 1938. They were in a sad state before being filled in when the first three-quarters of a mile was drained in 1964 and filled in. An old map shows that there were basins from the terminus near Corporation Street to just south of Maudland Road Bridge. The small Water Lane Aqueduct was demolished and the area around it cleared. A further 100 yards were drained at Holme, near Kendal, and pipes inserted owing to leakage.

When the M6 motorway extension was projected, despite strenuous efforts by The Association for the Restoration of the Lancaster Canal (as the Lancaster Canal Trust then was) and other bodies interested in the canal as well as by various individuals, it was decided that there would be five culverts above and one below Tewitfield, instead of low bridges

Looking up the bed of the canal at Stainton Crossing Bridge before the start of the restoration work as detailed in Chapter 19

which would have permitted the canal's use by pleasure craft. This was done even though the cost of bridges would not have been crippling. There was a limited success in that it was proposed by the Ministry that Kellet Lane Bridge was to be demolished for the M6 and replaced by one of only 12 feet in width rather than the normal width, meaning that broader vessels, including some of the British Waterways maintenance vessels would not be able to pass beneath it. A special cruise took place on Sunday, 28 August 1966 with *Shelagh*, a former Leeds & Liverpool barge, sailing from Tewitfield with a crowd of passengers. Eventually, the Trust was able to persuade the authorities to change widths so as to allow the larger vessels pass through.

In the mid-1970s, on the construction of the Levens Link, the drained canal bed was cut through in two places near Hincaster Tunnel. The then reason for the water channel above Tewitfield was because the canal supplied water via a pipeline to the I.C.I. Plant at Thornton.

This period was probably the all time low in the history of the Lancaster Canal. Now the pipes at Holme have been removed and replaced by a concrete flume and it has been recommended that nothing further be done to hinder the eventual restoration of the canal north of Tewitfield.

1972 saw a Preston Guild, held once every twenty years. That year, the Lancaster Canal Trust, the Lancaster Canal Boat Club and the Inland Waterways Association organised a rally celebrating both the Guild and the restoration of the Ashton Basin and also saving the last mile of canal in Preston. It had been proposed by the Central Lancashire New Town Corporation that the line of the canal from Haslam Park to its terminus at Aqueduct Street be used for a planned road to Ingol. At the time that was planned, it was very rarely that vessels sailed south of Woodplumpton Road, the main one being *Shelagh*, a former Leeds and Liverpool boat that did sailings from Haslam Park at that time and needed the basin entrance for turning. The towpath was in bad condition, the basin itself occupied by tree and bush growth, and the canal used as a rubbish tip. However, someone was found who wanted to make the basin useable again for moorings and, with help from the British Waterways Board (BWB), it was cleared out. With the canal again seeing some use, the threat of the road receded.

Work was done at clearing out the basin and by July 1974 it was receiving some use. There were improvements to the towpath and the land backing onto the houses. However, it was to be many years before the area was improved to its appearance as it is today on the stretch from the terminus to Haslam Park, and it receive the general use it now enjoys.

Looking up the canal by Ashton Basin

1976 saw a decision by the British Waterways Board (the then owners of the canal to Stainton) to allow powered craft to use the canal above Tewitfield Locks, the first time for nearly twenty years.

A link between the Lancaster Canal and the Leeds and Liverpool Canal by water had long been a dream. The original intention had, of course, been to build a huge aqueduct over the Ribble, but the costs of spanning the Lune meant that this had never happened. The possibilities of using Savick Brook to get down to the River Ribble, sail across it to the River Douglas and up it to join the Leeds and Liverpool Canal at Tarleton had long been proposed. In 1979 John Whittaker of Lancaster Canal Boat Club proposed a connecting link using Savick Brook. In 1984 the Ribble Link Trust was set up to promote the idea. There was a special Ribble Link Campaign Cruise under the auspices of the Ribble Link Trust in July 1988, it being planned to navigate from Tarleton to Preston Dock, stay the night, and then return. One craft sailed up Savick Brook to the Blackpool/Preston Road bridge, but this was only because the owner of the boat knew what he was doing. That cruise gained much more support for the campaign from the local authorities.

By 1990 the Ribble Link Trust was able to commission a feasibility study into the proposed link, but this fell through. A number of ups and downs followed. One idea was to have a 'landbridge' of boats being placed in a cradle at Lea Wharf (Bridge 18) and taken by low loader to Preston Dock, or the reverse of this. It was envisaged that this should be an interim measure. However, in 1995 things moved further forward with the application to Preston Borough Council to make a navigable waterway along Savick Brook from its confluence with the Ribble and to join the canal in Haslam Park. Originally it was proposed to utilise Sharoe Brook and Halsam Park for the Link, but considerable difficulties with land ownership and permissions resulted in the route actually taken.

In October 1997 it was anticipated that work on the construction of The Link would commence the following February. However, negotiations between Ribble Link Construction and Operations Ltd, which was a partnership between the Ribble Link Trust and Lancashire County Council, and the Waterways Trust, were long drawn out. The programme was then for the main construction to commence with the lock works and excavating the channel during the spring and summer of 2001. The Link was to be open to boating in spring 2002. The Millennium Commission had agreed to fund the Link as a community project for a linear water park.

The Link has nine locks, of which the first three form a staircase. There then follow five normal locks and the rotating sea lock. That lock has a 'rising sector gate' which is lowered onto the bed of the brook during operation and then raised to hold in the water as the tide goes out. Fish passes have been constructed.

Unfortunately, the start of work at the lower end of the Link, as originally planned, was delayed by Foot and Mouth Disease restrictions following the outbreak of the disease in 2001. However, clearance work further up was started.

Work began on the construction of the locks. By the end of June 2001 much work was going on round by lock 4 with sheet driving taking place and its shape evident. February 2002 saw much more excavation having been done on locks 4 and 5. Both of these locks were built on dry ground at the sides of a meander in Savick Brook. The design of them involved driving four rows of interlocking piles into the ground. (Lock 6 is the only one built on the line of the Brook.) Work on the staircase was well under way with cement being poured in. The basin at the junction with the main line had been excavated. The first lock gates to be fitted, which had been built by the Northwich Works of British Waterways, were the upper pair at lock 5.

The Link is for vessels with a maximum length of 62 ft 0 in and a maximum breadth of 10 ft 6 in. August 2001 saw concern about a number of tight bends. As a result, there were trials with a 70 foot measuring rod. Following on from this, some of them had to be re-aligned.

During the time of the construction work, the weather played its part, causing flooding with some damage. By the end of June 2002 most of the works had been done. A coffer dam, which had been placed around the rotating sector gate at the bottom of the Link was removed. This lock, 9, is a rotating sea lock on the tidal section of Savick Brook below the Blackpool Road Bridge.

Care was taken to retain the original north bank of Savick Brook so as to conserve the existing flora and fauna. Down to lock 8 became a footpath and cycleway. There is no path beyond lock 8. Following the completion of the construction work, the south bank was quickly re-colonised by nature.

On Friday 12 July 2002 the first craft other than work boats used the Ribble Link. There had been some publicity as to when the boats would start the journey down the Link, full details having been given in the Spring 2002 edition of *Waterwitch*, the journal of the Lancaster Canal Trust, and which was taken from the Ribble Link website. A VIP flotilla was due to arrive at the junction at 10.00 am for an opening ceremony and begin sailing down the Link at 10.15 am prompt. Unfortunately, the timings had been changed and several people, including the author,

Waterwitch, the Lancaster Canal Trust's trip boat, moored at Crooklands

were not aware of this. As a result, they turned up to see the first cruisers set off down the locks only to find that there were none around. Enquiries at the BWB point produced the information that they had gone. The BWB personnel pointed out that the Link was not yet officially open and seemed amazed that people expected to see boats on a canal, the first new navigation constructed in England since the Manchester Ship Canal over a hundred years earlier. (The official opening was not until the September when it was performed by the Rt Hon. Margaret Beckett, then Secretary of State for the Environment, Food and Rural Affairs.) Those first boats on the Link were all owned by members of the Ribble Link Trust. They made their way down the Link and up to Preston Docks, where many people were awaiting their arrival from the Lancaster Canal.

The launching of craft can now be done at Millness. The Lancaster Canal Trust has regular sailings on their craft, *Waterwitch*, from the Crooklands wharf in summer at weekends and for special events. They have also restored the Crooklands stables which, in 1993, were in a derelict state covered with a mass of ivy and fallen timbers.

Over the years, various works have been undertaken by the Lancaster Canal Trust with the Waterways Recovery Group and others. In June 1980 men from 2 Troop, 48 Field Squadron set to work on Hincaster Tunnel and horsepath. They cleared out the horsepath, which had by then become very overgrown and in poor condition, and cleared all the trees and undergrowth from the tunnel portals. Work has always had to be ongoing as otherwise the growth soon returns, such as by the steps down from the horsepath to the towpath by the East Portal of the Tunnel and along the horsepath itself. The stone wall by that lower horsepath has been rebuilt by volunteers.

Other works done have included restoration work on the Sedgwick Aqueduct, the restoration of a lock at Tewitfield, work on various bridges, and other maintenance tasks. Kendal Changeline and Natland Mill bridges have been restored with Heritage Lottery funding and assistance from Kendal Civic Society.

Work is taking place with the 'Towpath Trail' from Kendal through to Lancaster. This is to improve the towpath and make it more user friendly, including for those who are disabled.

More work has taken place under the auspices of the Lancaster Canal Trust at Stainton, this being known as 'The First Furlong' (see Chapter 19). Here, a short stretch of canal has been largely restored between Stainton Crossing Bridge and Sellet Hall Bridge, but further work has to be done before it is watered and the bund removed. Hopefully, it is just the first step of the way to returning to Kendal. With some diversions plus an aqueduct near Hincaster, and removing the top lock at Tewitfield to above the culvert under the M6, it is technically possible to restore the Lancaster Canal. There have been a number of occasions when it has been the expectation of the work going ahead in three phases, only for delays by development proposals in Kendal and obtaining funding dashing the scheme yet again.

CHAPTER 8

The Lune Aqueduct

T HE MOST CELEBRATED architectural feature of the Lancaster Canal is the Lune Aqueduct designed by John Rennie. It was his first major commission for bridging a watercourse. It is 600 feet in length and 60 feet high, with five 70-foot semi-circular arches supported on rustic pillars with Gothic ends. It is topped by a massive cornice and the parapet is partly balustraded. The aqueduct is the first one for which Rennie used the inverted arch principle, something not visible. Extra strength was provided and exploding arches prevented by building an inverted arch in contact with the other arches where they were most likely to burst outwards with the weight of the cornice. The spandrels, the triangular parts between the arches, hide the inverted arches.

Originally it was estimated that the aqueduct would cost £18,618 16*s*. 0*d*., an amount subsequently amended to £27,500. Rennie favoured brick but the committee preferred stone, so as to match how Georgian Lancaster was built. When commenting on the tenders for the masonry, Rennie compared the Lune Aqueduct with brick-built ones on the canals in the Midlands. He wrote to Gregson '… I still wish the Committee had tried brick, it would have saved many thousands of pounds.'

The contractors appointed for the construction of the aqueduct were Alexander Stevens and Son of Edinburgh, the contract being ratified by the Committee in June 1793 and sealed on 26 July. By 20 August the masons had laid the first stone of the aqueduct. In January 1794, Millar, the resident engineer, started the pile-driving within deep coffer dams which had been sunk into the river bed. The dams were pumped dry by steam-pumps, an engine house having been built. In January 1794, William Cartwright was appointed assistant resident engineer and given special responsibility for the foundations. Work on the coffer dams was not going as well as intended by May that year. This was of concern to Rennie, Millar, Cartwright and the committee. As a result, the Canal Company took over the work on the foundations of the piers from Stevens, who apparently agreed to this without argument.

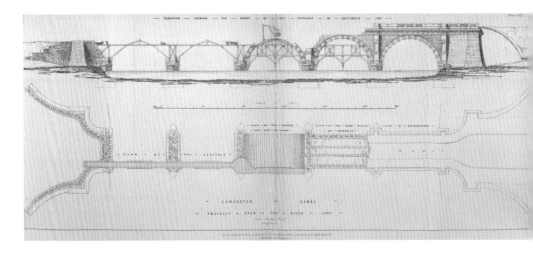

Construction of the Lune Aqueduct: 'Elevation shewing the works as they appeared in September 1795', Day and Haghe Lithograph, 1 January 1837. Image courtesy of the Institution of Civil Engineers, ICE Library.

By July there were one hundred and fifty men working day and night. Troubles arose through drunken engine attendants, the flooding of the coffer dams owing to sudden rises in the level of the river, bad weather and recalcitrant workmen. The piles they made are about 20 feet long, 1 foot wide and 6 inches deep, making a very solid base for the foundations to the piers. Timber came from what is now Klaipeda in Lithuania. The piers, from the foundation 20 feet below the level of Skerton Weir, are rectangular to the bed of the river and then have Gothic arches to 2 feet 6 inches above the springs of the aqueduct arches. Cartwright informed the Committee that work on the foundations was to be continued with all urgency with double lots of men working night and day.

In July 1795, in spite of the problems, the piers were complete. They had cost £14,792 9s. 8¼d. (this was after selling off surplus materials and machinery, including the steam engines.) Cartwright was presented with a silver cup costing £17 7s. (£17.35) 'as a reward for his extra care in superintending the Foundations of the Lune Aqueduct.' The committee also gave themselves a justifiable pat on the back; 'Although the cost has been considerable the Committee trust that succeeding ages will give credit and have reason to boast of the permanency of that Work.'

Now they were able to proceed with the upper works which went ahead rapidly. The specifications give much detail of the stonework and the way in which the aqueduct was to be built. The arch stones were to be 4 feet long taken in the direction of the radius and not less than 1 foot thick and of no less than 2 feet in breadth. The outside walls between the arches were to be 5 feet in thickness, done in rustic work as high as the cornice, and built in courses not less than 1 foot thick. The wing walls up to the cornice were to be built of the same kind of rustic ashlar (square-cut, dressed stone) as the walls between the arches, and were to have a batter for strength. The mortar for the parts of the work above the water was to be one part of well-burnt unslaked lime and four to five parts of river sand in proper proportions of coarse and fine sand. The puddle for the water channel was to be a yard thick over the whole of the aqueduct. All this detail and more reveals how strongly constructed the aqueduct was to be.

However, Rennie was not satisfied that even this would be sufficient and proposed modifications to give additional strength. Alexander Stevens considered them unnecessary, on which point he received the backing of the committee. Stevens must have had a likeable, friendly nature as well as strong principles because when he died on 29 January 1796 at the age of sixty-six, both Rennie and Millar wrote movingly of his loss. Rennie was not able to attend the funeral and wrote 'I therefore with you sincerely drop a tear to his memory and, had my engagements been fewer than they are, would have been in Lancaster to assist at the funeral.' Following his father's death, Stevens' son completed the aqueduct. The last arch was finished in July 1797 and the whole completed in the autumn of the same year, having cost £48,320 18s. 10d. to build.

On the north-east side of the aqueduct is the inscription 'To Public Prosperity', whilst on the south-west side above the central arch is a Latin inscription which can be translated as follows:

Old needs are served; far distant sites combined;
Rivers by art to bring new wealth are joined.
A.D. 1797. J. Rennie, engineer. A. Stevens and Son, contractors.

The keystone on that arch has been carved to represent Lancaster Castle Gateway.

There is a memorial stone to Stevens in the south wall of Lancaster Priory Church.

On 13 September 1997, to commemorate its 200th Anniversary, the aqueduct was ceremonially re-opened. A flotilla of boats, led by *Raven* on which were the then Mayor of Lancaster and several costumed characters, including 'John Rennie' drew up at a tape spanning the water channel. Speeches were made, Mrs. Hilda Shuttleworth, the Mayor, cut the tape and the *Raven* led the flotilla over the aqueduct.

Early in the present century, it was appreciated that the Lune Aqueduct needed a lot of attention, both to the structure itself and to the areas around it. A number of the balustrades and copings were either loose or missing, there was considerable growth around some of the masonry, the water channel needed pointing work to cure leaks, and there was graffiti to be removed. In addition, better access between the Millennium Cycleway below and the towpath above was needed, vegetation needed to be managed, a new visitor car park provided on Caton Road, and various other works needed to be done. The canal had to be closed a number of times to allow first of all emergency remedial work and then the main works to be carried out, all this starting from March 2006 and continuing in stages over the following years. In 2010, the 'Lune Aqueduct, Lancaster Canal Conservation Management Plan' was produced by British Waterways, a very comprehensive and detailed study, resulting in the aqueduct and its surroundings, including a very pleasant recreation area just by the car park and connecting onto the bank of the Lune, as we see them today. The works were completed in 2012.

The Lune Aqueduct is Grade I listed. Britton, in *The Beauties of England and Wales*, wrote in 1807 that the aqueduct was considered 'the most magnificent structure of this kind that has been erected in Great Britain and may fairly vie with any of the pompous works of the Romans.' This still holds good today.

CHAPTER 9

The Packet Boats

IT WAS NOT LONG AFTER the Lancaster Canal was opened that the packet-boat service started. August 1798 saw the start of a service on the North End between Preston and Lancaster. The report of the General Meeting of Proprietors held on 1 January 1799 tells that the net produce to 1 December 1798 was about £200, which had been applied in payment for the large boat, Mr Brockbank having been engaged to build two Packet Boats, which were to be paid for from their own earnings. Brockbanks were major Lancaster ship builders at that time, their yard being where Sainsbury's now stands.

In the *Lancaster Gazette* for 25 July 1801, it was advertised that the packet boats between Preston and Lancaster 'will sail on Sunday morning next at 8 o'clock, and continue to set out every morning at the same hour.' In those days, sailing on the canal was considered an adventure. To help overcome this, an advert in 1802 for trips from Lancaster to Preston for the Preston Guild claimed that 'for safety, economy and comfort no other mode of conveyance could be so eligible; for there the timid might be at ease and the most delicate mind without fear.' From 3 September 1804 the packet boats changed their Preston terminus to the canal basin near the Chapel-yard, 'A situation so central and convenient to the town and trade of Preston' according to the notice of the change. 1 May 1820 saw the packet-boat service extended to Kendal, in competition with the turnpike coaches. The service was advertised to leave Preston at 6.00 a.m., arrive at Lancaster at 1.00 p.m. and the Tewitfield Locks at 4.00 p.m. Kendal was reached at 8.00 p.m., in time for the passengers to catch the stage coach for the north. The fares for the whole journey were 6s. in the fore cabin and 4s. in the aft cabin. Refreshments, tea and coffee were served on board.

In the year to 31 December 1818, the last full year before the opening of the canal through to Kendal, the Packet Boats made a profit of £232 6s. 2d. (see table 2). However, in 1819 there was no profit from the Packet Boats and only £43 profit in 1820. The reports to the Annual General Meetings for those two years reveal that low fares charged by coaches

Dukes Bridge and former Duke inn, Farleton

and considerable repairs to the old boats had led to debt in the first year of the canal running through to Kendal. Those debts had been paid off in the second year. The 1820 report went on to say of six months during which the Packet Boats sailed the whole canal from Preston to Kendal, 'this arrangement has been more productive, and has afforded greater accommodation to the public'.

Starting in 1826 there was an additional boat on Mondays to Saturdays, leaving Lancaster at 6.00 a.m. and reaching Preston at noon. It returned at 2.00 p.m. and arrived back in Lancaster at 8.00 p.m. By then the Preston–Kendal boat times had apparently been changed to 7.00 a.m., as an advertisement in the 25 February 1826 issue of the *Lancaster Gazette* states that they would sail at 7.00 a.m. as usual.

The February 1828 General Meeting reported a 'great falling off' in the receipts of the packet boats owing to reduced fares of the stage coaches. By the 1830s, the threat of the railways was looming, and there was still competition from the stage coaches. The February 1833 General Meeting reports that the Committee had determined to try a 'quick sailing Passage Boat between Lancaster and Preston similar to those on the Ardrossan Canal.' If this service proved a success, it would be extended to Kendal, with some improvements to the Tewitfield locks. As a result, in 1833 the Swift Boat service was introduced.

The first vessel used on this service was *Water Witch*, an iron-hulled vessel obtained from Mr W. Houston of Paisley in January 1833. She was 76 feet in length, had a 6 foot beam and could carry one hundred and twenty passengers. A time sheet shows that the service between Preston and Lancaster commenced on 1 April 1833. This vessel was improved in 1835. The service through to Kendal from Preston sailed on alternate days, the return journey being made the following day. On Mondays, Wednesdays and Fridays the packet left Kendal at 6.00 a.m., arrived in Lancaster at 1.00 p.m., and Preston shortly after 4.00 p.m. On Tuesdays, Thursdays and Saturdays the return journey started from Preston at 9.30 a.m., reached Lancaster at 1.00 p.m., and Kendal at 7.30 p.m. There were no changes in the fares. This swift service was only possible because of there being no locks until Tewitfield. Also, apart from short stretches in Lancaster and Kendal, the towpath was on the same side of the canal for the whole journey. An average of 10 miles per hour to Lancaster was achieved. The boats were horse-drawn, so stables had to be built at eleven horse-changing points. Boathouses were built at Preston, Lancaster and Kendal, and a passenger shed was built at Preston.

On 22 July 1833 the Swift Boat service was extended through to Kendal. Apparently the 57-mile journey was done in seven hours, the two horses being changed every four miles. The fares were unchanged and sixteen thousand passengers made journeys in the first six months. Sometimes passengers on the express boats had to disembark at the foot of the locks, walk up, and board a boat waiting at the top (similarly for the return journey from Kendal to Lancaster). However, some boats went straight through the locks, with passengers staying on board if they chose to. There is some discrepancy regarding dates as a letter from London and North Western Railway dated 17 December 1912 shows Lancaster and Preston sailings commencing from 20 May 1833 and Kendal to Preston sailings from 9 July 1833. In Preston, there were omnibuses between the Packets and the Railway and coaches to and from Bolton and Chorley met the Packets at Canal Wharf.

The new service proved popular and in March 1834 a second boat, the *Swiftsure*, joined the *Water Witch*. This was an iron-hulled vessel built by Thomas Vernon and Co. of Liverpool. The woodwork for the boat was put together at the Canal workshops in Lancaster. August 1835 saw a third boat, *Swallow*, join the fleet, but no details of this vessel are known.

The iron hull of a fourth boat was ordered in 1839 from Mr McDowell of Glasgow and named *Crewdson* after the chairman of the Company. In later years this vessel was renamed *Water Witch II* and was eventually used as a canal inspection boat for many years. The cabin had by then been shortened, and later placed in storage. It lay on display on the canal bank near Aldcliffe Road until 1929, when it was broken up. A replica is on display in the Lancaster Maritime Museum.

Crewdson arrived ready for additional services from June 1839 when there were three sailings each way between Lancaster and Preston, two of them going through to Kendal. Fares were 3*s.* in the fore cabin and 2*s.* in the aft cabin between either Kendal and Lancaster or Lancaster and Preston. Omnibuses ran between the canal and the railway at Preston and timings were arranged so as to connect with trains for Manchester and Liverpool. In addition coaches met the packet boats at the canal wharf in Preston, taking passengers to and from Chorley and Bolton.

On the opening of the railway to Lancaster, the Lancaster Canal Company halved their fares to 1*s.* 6*d.* and 1*s.* In wintertime the boats were heated and refreshments continued to be provided on board. Travelling was smooth and comfortable and no passengers were lost to the railway, despite their cut rate fare of 4*s.* for a combined rail and coach journey to Kendal. *Bradshaw* (the railway timetable) for 1842 includes the connecting times for the packet-boat services between Lancaster and Kendal. The service between Lancaster and Preston was promptly withdrawn, however, when the Company took over the Lancaster and Preston Junction Railway!

From 1 September 1842, sailings between Lancaster and Kendal left at 7.30 a.m. and noon. The journeys from Kendal left at 8.30 a.m. and 1.30 p.m. A free omnibus service was provided for the short journey between the packet station and the railway station in Lancaster, where the boats connected with the trains.

A story is told of a near-sighted old lady who wished to make a fifteen mile journey to Lancaster so as to arrive in the town as early as possible. Some time after boarding the packet, observing that there was no movement, she asked a member of the crew when the boat was going to start for Lancaster. She was told 'Why missis, ye are theer now; come on oot.'

Two horses were used on the Swift Boat service; the postilion, usually a boy, rode on the second one and drove the first. The boy was obliged to stoop quite low on the horse's neck to pass under the low arches of the bridges. The speed of the boat was regulated by the helmsman, who was known as the 'conductor' or 'master', by giving a blast on a whistle if the boy was going too slowly. Postilions were changed at Lancaster.

The packet-boat services ceased on 22 September 1846, on the opening of the Lancaster and Carlisle Railway's line to Kendal. In 1865, B. P. Gregson wrote that 'In 1833 the Swift Passenger Boats were established and worked to profit until the Lancaster and Preston Junction Railway was opened in 1840, and thence maintained a successful opposition to the railway till September 1842 ...' Gregson himself had been the one largely responsible for the establishment and the success of the Swift Boat service.

It is believed that the original *Water Witch* and the *Swiftsure* were transferred to the Crinan Canal before 1856.

Carnforth coke ovens

CHAPTER 10

Coke Ovens

DURING THE UPDATING OF THIS VOLUME, more information has been found about coke ovens, or cinder ovens as they are sometimes called, on the Lancaster Canal. This follows on from the setting up of the 'Friends of Carnforth Coke Ovens', of whom the author is the treasurer. Many people have thought that those at Carnforth were the remains of lime kilns, but coke ovens are of a very different construction and built for a different purpose than the former. Lime kilns were loaded from the top whilst coke ovens were loaded from the front.

The beehive-shaped coke ovens were constructed of brick, usually in batteries of three or more, in a number of places along the canal. They provided coke for use by local industries, such as blacksmiths and bakeries, and domestically. These ovens probably remained in use until the second half of the nineteenth century. Those known to have existed or still remaining on the Lancaster Canal were all on the non-towpath side. Coal was sealed into them and converted by heat into coke. One oven would be being loaded and sealed. Another oven would be heated and converting coal to coke. A third oven would be cooling down.

The process of making coke in these ovens was by first loading the coking coal into the oven. This was a coal low in gas content and high in carbon content. The oven was lighted and sealed. The impurities in the coal were burned off, such as gas, leaving the purified carbon. Very little oxygen was able to enter an oven and there was a small flue at the top for the gases to escape, resulting in the carbon being left behind. Coke was a smokeless fuel and in later years was a by product of the production of town gas, with the result that heaps of coke were to be seen outside gasworks in the twentieth century. It was used by blacksmiths and bakers as well as domestically and heated offices in smokeless zones, such as central Lancaster. In its latter days, coke was known as sunbrite and came in three sizes, singles which were about half an inch across, doubles which were used domestically, and trebles. Following the demise of town gas, there is hardly any coke manufactured now, and coal merchants have not sold it for around twenty years.

Holme coke ovens

As reported in the *Lancaster Gazette*, there was an enquiry held in Lancaster Town Hall in September 1831 into the conduct of Mr Pye who was the assistant overseer of the poor. He had refused tickets for two down and outs for accommodation with the result that they had sought to spend the night in a lime-kiln near the canal not far from the Lune aqueduct. Unfortunately they had been overcome by fumes and died there, resulting in the enquiry. One of the witnesses, Lancaster watch-maker Mr J. Gregson, a witness speaking in favour of Mr Pye, told that it was usual practice for those claiming financial assistance 'to obtain money if they could, and then go to cinder ovens to sleep. He had been informed that great numbers slept at the ovens at Tewitfield'.

Known details of coke ovens by the canal:

Ellel (Galgate): Ovens in a former quarry to the south of Double Bridge 85, their number is not known. Not obviously visible from the canal towpath.

Lancaster: This is a bank of at least four and probably originally five ovens. They are on land at the present used by Lansil Golf Club and are by the bend in the canal immediately on the city side of the Bulk Aqueduct. A lot of clearance work has now been done around the ovens and down to the canal wharf at which the coal would be landed. At the present, they may not be visible from the towpath in the summer months because of all the scrub growth which springs up in front of them and by the canal. They are on a bank a short way above the canal, close to a track.

Bolton-le-Sands: The ovens are remembered by the name of Bridge 125, Bolton Cinder Ovens. The ovens are marked on the 1846 6 inch Ordnance Survey map and are referred to in a list of rentals of Canal Company lands for 1817. Work has been started to try to find whether anything of the structures remains. Pieces of stone and brick, which have clearly been cut and shaped, have been unearthed. A section of what appears to be a side wall has been exposed and the floor of one oven found.

Carnforth: This bank of five ovens is to the south of Thwaite End Bridge 127 and shown on early maps. The ovens are referred to in the list of rentals of 1817. Work has been done clearing the scrub around them so that they are better seen. A sturdy fence has been erected around them and work has been done at exposing the edge of the adjacent wharf. The backs of these ovens are visible from the towpath. They can be passed by following the public footpath between bridges 125 and 127, which is part of the original turnpike road from Garstang to Heron Syke near Burton. Work has been done on exposing the wharf. It is intended that further work will be done on this site.

Tewitfield: The remains of the ovens are in private grounds adjacent to the Longlands Hotel. An advertisement in the *Westmorland Advertiser and Kendal Chronicle* for 7 August 1813 shows that the whole or part of a Concern on the Lancaster Canal was for sale by private treaty. It consisted of 'Three excellent Canal Boats with Eight Cinder Ovens, eligibly situated at Tewitfield'. The length of the wall at the back of the site shows where they all were. Now, just one still remains. At one stage it was used to house chickens. The oven is not visible from the canal.

Holme: Four ovens remain here and that may have been the original number. They appear to be in two pairs of slightly different design. The right hand oven, when seen from by the canal, has been dug out, exposing the smooth brick floor. The ovens are visible from on the canal towpath, where there is an interpretation board.

Crooklands: A document regarding these ovens has recently been discovered in the archives of Civil Engineers in London. It is dated 26 April 1822 and shows 'Expence of Building Six Cinder Ovens at Crooklands'. Charles Airey was paid £16 for his labour of building 4 ovens plus £2 10s. 8d. for other work relating to them. John Dawson was paid £8 for building 2 ovens plus £1 7s. 0d. for other work. J. B. Stainton was paid £9 5s. 0d. for smith work. The whole cost of the ovens, including the above labour, materials and transport, came to £107 10s. 7d.

Kendal: Hoggarth's map of 1853 shows that there was a bank of five ovens just to the south of Changeline bridge. The site of these ovens is now under the school sports field.

CHAPTER 11

Snippets

1   Where the canal was cut through a watertight soil, such as clay, no lining was necessary. Everywhere else the canal bed was lined or 'puddled'. Puddling was a mass of earth which had been reduced to a semi-fluid state by working it with a spade, water being mixed in until the mass was rendered uniform. It was so condensed that water could only pass through it very slowly, if at all. A lightish loam mixed with a coarse sand or fine gravel made the best puddling stuff. This mixture was then spread in layers over the excavated channel, the final thickness being anything from 18 inches to 3 feet according to the porosity of the soil. This in turn was covered with an 18 inch layer of soil or poorer clay. Once it had been lined the canal had to be filled with water quickly before it could be damaged by hot weather drying it out.

2.   The modern term 'navvy' derives from the building of the canals when labourers, often Irishmen, were known as 'navigators'

3.   Rennie's standard bridges, common on the main line from Preston to Tewitfield, are all of the same basic design. The walls curve inwards in plan between buttressed piers at each side of the canal and are battered to give added strength. Below the parapet there is a projecting string course. Although they are called 'standard' it is probable that no two are completely identical. All of the 'standard' bridges had a white band painted round the arch to make them more visible to boatmen.

4.   Rennie's 'little aqueducts' are all of the same basic design with modifications as dictated by the problems of the individual sites. The aqueducts have walls which are curved sharply inwards in plan between buttresses at each end. In order to resist the pressure of the water channel they are strongly battered outwards.

5.   At various points along the canal, normally a mile apart but some are now missing, are milestones which show the distance from Preston,

Garstang, Lancaster or Kendal. When approaching a milestone, the distance seen is that from the nearest one of those places behind, and not the distance to the one in front. This sometimes causes people not familiar with this some confusion. This was for assistance in billing for carriage, showing how far the goods had been brought, and ensured that the full toll was paid by carriers. There are two styles of milestone, those with a plaque and the name of the town left and those with the just the distance engraved on them, these being above Lancaster. Sometimes a plaque, or both plaques, is missing. Some milestones have a benchmark on top of them. In a number of places there are smaller stones set facing the canal, but with no distances on them. These indicate the half mile between two milestones. As part of the bicentenary celebrations of 2019, Canal & River Trust and the Lancaster Canal Trust have joined together with Lancaster sculptor Alan Ward to restore the missing milestones.

6.   There were several accidents on the tramroad bridge, which was situated at the foot of a steep incline. The wagons were attached to an endless chain which was worked by a stationary steam engine at the top of Avenham Inclined Plane. On 3 October 1826 the chain broke and the wagons on it at the time ran away, killing two horses under the charge of John Roberts of Walton Summit, an employee of Hall and Company, Canal Traders. Apparently a team belonging to Lord Balcarres, a colliery owner, had landed at the engine when the chain snapped near it and fell into the catches of their unhooked wagon, dragging it down the hill. At the time Roberts' foremost wagon (he was moving six in three teams of two horses and two wagons each) was in the middle of the incline. The driver leapt from the wagon and Lord Balcarres' wagon passed by without hurting either him or the horses which were going up the roadside. Roberts' second wagon, which had gone a little way up the hill, passed its two horses, but the wagon from the middle of the hill caught in their gears and dragged them backwards towards the bridge. Lord Balcarres' wagon went over them, crashed through the bridge handrail and fell into the River Ribble. One of the horses was killed immediately, the other, in trying to rise, fell over the bridge onto the rocks in the river and was killed. Hall and Company's compensation claim was rejected as Roberts had infringed a by-law by attaching one wagon to the endless chain before the preceding wagon had been detached at the top, the rule being that only one wagon was to be raised or lowered at a time. In 1976 the wagon from the tramroad was found in the mud on the bed of the Ribble having laid there for one hundred and fifty years since this accident.

7.   1976 was one of the few times when there was a serious water shortage in the canal, its level being reduced by nearly a foot. Another major water shortage was one hundred and fifty years before this. On 25 August 1826, the Lancaster Canal Company records show that packets could not sail in the North End due to low water levels. Earlier in the month the canal was closed from Tewitfield Locks to Holme, where it was found that the bottom was in bad condition. On 29 August 1826, traffic on the canal was suspended because of the exceptionally dry weather, a situation aggravated by a burst in Killington Reservoir.

8.   It is said that Archibald Millar, who was a surveyor under Rennie, calculated his levels incorrectly at Brock. As a result, Rennie designed a tunnel beneath the river. He requested that Eastburn check the levels, resulting in the mistake being discovered.

9.   In 1974 Bath Mill, which was by the canal at Lancaster, was demolished. During demolition of the tower extension a beer bottle was found cemented into the tower about a yard from the top. Inside was a message written in good copperplate writing on yellowing paper: 'This tower was built by four masons and five labourers in the year 1897. Names below: Alfred Grice, Thomas Harrison, Roger Helm, William Thompson, Thomas Eccles, Edward Hock, Thomas Airey, James Dowthwaite, Joseph Hurst, Thomas Armstrong, drink success to the man who found this bottle.' The area where the mill was is now housing.

10.   During the Second World War, a length of the canal in the Glasson area and to the south of there was a part of an official stop-line to contain any invasion from the Irish Sea. That is why some bridges have had the stonework removed down to the string courses and why some, such as bridge 6 on the Glasson Arm have large concrete blocks at the end. The author will be grateful if anyone can let him have any further information about this stop line as he has found very little information.

11.   During World War II, water was taken from the canal at Hest Bank to fill the troughs on the railway.

12.   It is on record that in 1889 the drinking water for Glasson was drawn from the canal basin.

13.   Occasionally a stretch of water is coloured with dye when the engineers are checking for leaks (there have been times when the whole

bank had given way!) In June 1858, workmen repairing the Roebuck Culvert, 12 miles from Preston, noticed that the water was flowing towards Preston and that the level of the canal had fallen. It was found that the bank had given way at Salwick Moss, 6.5 miles from Preston. Stopgates were put in at Swillbrook, 1.5 miles north, and at Hollinshead Fold, 2 miles south. 60 yards of embankment had given way. Preston mills were cut off from their supplies as a result of the loss of water.

14.   During World War II there was a Canal (Defence) Advisory Committee, but the military left the Lancaster alone.

15.   The paper used for copy letters during World War II reveals economy and paper saving. The backs of old correspondence were used. One letter from the Lancaster dated 10 October 1941 is on a letter dated 6 July 1904 from Chaffer and Brundenberg Limited of Manchester, to the Chief Mechanical Engineer of the Lancashire and Yorkshire Railway about an enquiry for pressure gauges.

16.   In 1942 there was correspondence on the maximum number of boats which could be operated on the Lancaster Canal. Between Preston and Lancaster it was decided on forty making return trips, each week. Twenty-four were allowed to use Tewitfield Locks once a week. The same number could use the Glasson flight twice a week. Only the London, Midland and Scottish Railway Company's boats had used the Glasson Arm in the last ten years, so much draining was needed.

17.   Winter caused problems on the canal and there was wartime corre-spondence on the subject. The ice was broken by towing the engineer's barge, loaded at the stern so that the bows were out of the water. As many horses as possible were used to drag the boat, but it was not very satis-factory as the canal kept refreezing due to heavy frosts. On 6 February 1945 the ice-breaking boat sank at Garstang, closing the canal for a few hours. Traffic on the canal did not justify an increase in the number of ice-breaking vessels.

18.   A work-book for December 1842 shows that employees were working a six-day week. Pay ranged from 2*s.* to 3*s.* 6*d.*, the most common amount being 3*s.* 2*d.*, presumably per day. Jobs were varied covering repairs to locks, works on barrows and Thurnham Mill waterwheel.

19.　Water was fed into the canal from various sources beside the main Killington feeder. One generous supplier was a Mr Fielding at Calder. According to a letter from Cartwright of 5 July 1789, Mr Fielding gave the Lancaster Canal Company permission to take water from the Calder and 'should always be extremely willing to give the Canal Company as much water as he possibly could, not injuring his own work.' He also gave permission for all water to be taken from the Calder on Fridays. In 1799 Cartwright suggested that the Keer and the Brock be taken in to provide supplies of water for the canal, at about one tenth the cost of repuddling. This was not done.

20.　The wasting of water was a serious offence. Thomas Henry Burrow of Gleeston, near Ulverston, published a Public Apology on 16 March 1886 saying, 'I wantonly and foolishly opened a Clough in a Lockgate in Glasson Lockage, which resulted in a waste of water, and for such offence have rendered myself liable to a penalty of Five Pounds, or not less than Forty Shillings (two pounds), and in default of the payment of the Penalty, to imprisonment in the House of Correction for not exceeding Six Months nor less than Three Months'. He then went on to apologise for the offence and hope that the Canal Proprietors would not prosecute him.

21.　Another offence was bathing in the canal, mainly because bathers could easily swim to boats and steal from them. Three youths caught bathing were threatened with 'Prosecution, do agree to make this Public Submission, pay all expenses, and Promise not to offend again, in consequence of Legal Proceedings being stayed.' The youths each signed the submission which was witnessed by Inspector McClaren.

22.　There are pictures showing that the canal was also used for leisure purposes. One popular event was a Sunday School outing from Kendal to Sedgwick. A photograph of the well-cleaned boat shows it as being packed with people in their Sunday attire, probably overloaded. Another picture taken at Cottam Hall shows a boat definitely overcrowded with about 200 people crammed into it.

23.　A syphon, such as the two on the Lancaster Canal, works by taking the stream down beneath the canal and up again to a slightly lower level. The water enters a pool upstream of the canal, drops down beneath the canal bed, then passes into the pool downstream of the canal which is slightly lower than the other pool. This lower pool constantly overflows into the stream bed owing to the pressure of the water coming from upstream.

24. Most of the bridges throughout the length of the canal are officially named, but local names can be very different. The official names of bridges 122 to 125 in Bolton-le-Sands are Bolton Church Bridge, Bolton Turnpike Bridge, Chorley's Bridge and Bolton Cinder Ovens Bridge. Locally, these are often known as Boys' School Bridge, Packet Bridge, Walkden's Bridge (after John Walkden and his family who lived in a now long demolished cottage by the bridge) or Surgery Cottage Bridge (from the long ago days when the local doctor had his surgery by there), and Thwaite Brow (or just Brow) Bridge. All the bridges to 172, Stainton Crossing, have a number plate, generally on both sides. Kendal Changeline Bridge also has a number plate, 186. British Waterways introduced the numbering owing to the difficulty of knowing to which bridge people were referring when giving a name that was different from the one they knew.

25. The canal abounds with wildlife, in the water, beside the banks and in the air above. Apart from many common birds, the kingfisher is also sometimes seen darting above the water, as are terns (particularly along the Glasson Arm). Herons may be put to flight, particularly north of Lancaster and along to the end of the watered stretch of canal at Stainton. Waterfowl use the canal, particularly mallard and mute swans, both of which tend to favour stretches of water where people come to feed them, but can be seen anywhere. There are also moorhens, coot and shelducks to be seen and occasionally goosanders visit. Various insects, including damselfly and dragonfly, are around in the summer. Fish caught by anglers include perch, pike, roach and freshwater eels. Shoals of stick-lebacks are often to be seen. Sadly, the water vole is now rarely spotted. However, otters are now sometimes to be seen.

26. There are many varieties of flowers along the banks, such as meadowsweet, yellow flag, water lilies, water mint and many more hedgerow plants. Some areas are particularly lush with plant life, mainly those not walked as often. For the naturalist there is always something of interest to be seen around the canal.

27. There are a number of plantings, particularly of larch, by the canal. The original plantings were to provide timber for work connected with the canal. When stop planks were needed or timber for other purposes, larches could be felled locally rather than obtain materials from several miles away.

28. On many bridges there are ropemarks to be seen, these occurred when the ropes towing the boats rubbed against the sides of the bridges as a corner was turned. Holes can be seen in a number of bridges from when an iron plate or a wooden roller on the towpath side was fixed to protect the corner against wear.

29.   In many places along the canal, particularly on the offside, there are London and North Western Railway boundary posts. There is also a stud boundary marker for roadways, but there are not many of these to be seen. One is in the footpath in St Michael's Lane, Bolton-le-Sands below Bridge 122, Bolton Church Bridge. Another is near the dock at Glasson Dock.

30.   From time to time stretches of the canal have to be drained for repair work to be undertaken. In December 1988 part of the canal was drained in Lancaster and an unexploded shell under Penny Street Bridge came into sight. A policeman guarded it until a bomb disposal unit from Liverpool arrived to deal with it.

31.   The coming of the canal must have caused a major upheaval in various towns and villages along its line. Nowhere must this have been more so than in Bolton-le-Sands. There the Town End part of the village had its road up to the parish church cut through. A new road had to be built round the other side of the canal to link the two parts of the village together again. What is now Packet Lane was once part of the main street, but this too was cut and the present road to its left and over the bridge built instead. From Packet Hill, which had to be constructed, houses on what was the road before the coming of the canal can be seen below, the fronts of them formerly facing onto the now non-existent road. A London and North Western Railway boundary stone is still to be found at the bottom of the hill, just below the post office.

32.   At a number of points along the canal are plugs for use if necessary to drain a section of the canal, such as if there is a leak. In a few places there are the remains of a windlass, which does not seem to be at a spot to serve a useful purpose. These were for use in drawing out a plug.

33.   Finally, if the Lancaster Canal is of interest to you, why not join the Lancaster Canal Trust? For details, visit www.lctrust.co.uk.

Holme Mills

PART TWO

Walking the Canal

Lock 1, Ribble Link

Introduction

THE TOWPATH AND THE PUBLIC FOOTPATH on the Kendal section are generally in good condition. Footwear suitable for any normal public footpath can be worn. Much of the towpath has been resurfaced, but not the Glasson Dock Arm or some parts above Tewitfield, and can be used by cyclists. It is only in wet weather, when the path can be very muddy in places, and frosty conditions when it can be very slippery, that any real problems are likely to be encountered. As it is level, the towpath can be used by virtually anybody able to get outside and walk a little. There are facilities for access by people who are disabled to join the towpath at a number of points.

Walking the towpath can be done in long or short stages, just as desired. There are many walks along its length which can be done as a round trip involving another path or road or visit to a village. As a rough guide, allow for walking at about 2.5 miles an hour in normal conditions. However, it is easy to take much longer if so inclined with looking at the scenery, watching activities, etc.

From the original basin in Preston to Canal Head in Kendal is 57 miles, however allowance needs to be made for the distance from the canal to the town or village centre. Mileages for the sections as set out in the book, and which are based on the milestones plus distance to town or village centres, are:

Preston to Bilsborrow	12.5 miles	20 kilometres
Bilsborrow to Garstang	5.5 miles	8.75 kilometres
Garstang to Galgate	8.75 miles	14 kilometres
Galgate to Lancaster	4.75 miles	7.5 kilometres
Lancaster to Carnforth	8.5 miles	13.5 kilometres

Carnforth to Tewitfield	4.25 miles	6.75 kilometres
Tewitfield to Holme	4 miles	6.5 kilometres
Holme to Hincaster	8 miles	12.75 kilomtres
Hincaster to Kendal	6 miles	9.5 kilometres
Galgate to Glasson	3 miles	4.75 kilomtres

Millennium Ribble Link 5.5–6.5 miles 8.75–10.5 km.

Circular walks can also be done involving both the main line and the Ribble Link. For ease of description, it is assumed that the reader will be starting from Haslam Park.

For the first walk, go westwards from Haslam Park to the junction with the Ribble Link and turn down it to Goodier Bridge. If desired, then go down the short stretch beyond to Lock 8 before turning back and

Canal by outlet and Haslam Park

crossing the bridge. At its far end on the right there is a stile into the field. Go diagonally right up the field to the top, by the pylon lines, where a stile by the gate leads into another field. Go up the field on its right-hand side, passing a pylon, and at its top is another stile by a gate. Cross it onto the road in front of houses and a farm. Turn right and follow the road round to its junction with Darkinsor Lane on the right.

Go down the lane, across a railway bridge and come to Bridge 19, Harrisons, over the canal and there go down the steps onto the towpath. Turn right and continue along the towpath, passing the junction to the Millennium Ribble Link, until the starting point is reached.

For a longer walk which incorporates seeing the rotating lock, go westwards from Haslam Park and continue along the main line of the canal to where it swings right at Bridge 25, Wilsons, at Salwick. There, leave the towpath and go down the short stretch of roadway leading to another road. Turn left. Follow this road straight along, over the railway, past the works, and straight along through Clifton to Blackpool Road. Turn left along it on its right-hand side, come to Savick Bridge, and look down to the lock. Continue on along the road for a short distance, having crossed over the road, pass the bus stop, and come to a stile. Cross the stile and go straight up the track to Goodier Bridge, then turn right up the Link. At the top of the Link, turn right along the main line to your starting point.

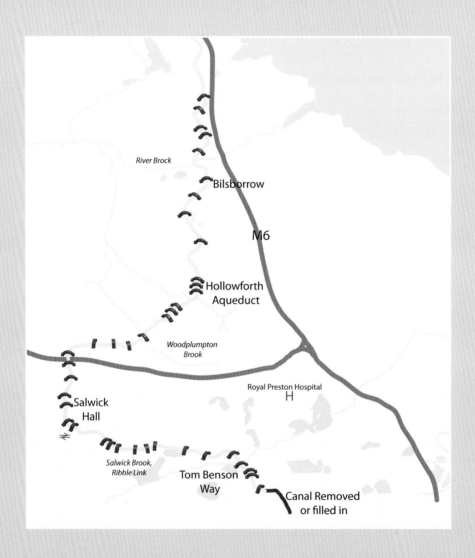

River Brock

Bilsborrow

M6

Hollowforth
Aqueduct

Woodplumpton
Brook

Royal Preston Hospital
H

Salwick
Hall

Salwick Brook,
Ribble Link

Tom Benson
Way

Canal Removed
or filled in

CHAPTER 12

Preston to Bilsborrow

THE NORTH END OF THE LANCASTER CANAL started originally from behind Corporation Street in Preston, but this part has now virtually all been cleared. To reach the present day terminus go down Corporation Street from opposite Debenhams, across some pedestrian crossings to where Aldi is straight in front. Turn right and then left to pass along the side of Aldi, which is on the site of the old goods warehouses. Continue along the road, to the University of Central Lancashire, which has a number of buildings. Cross over Kendal Street, a canal reminder, and pass Foster College which partly stands on the site of vanished canal basins. Then turn left into Maudland Road and across the railway bridge. From the bridge, looking northwards, the site of the canal is all filled in apart from a few yards just seen under another

End of canal, Preston

Ashton Basin

railway bridge that carried a line going east. Take the next turning right (Maudland Bank) to Fylde Road and then turn left and pass under the West Coast Main Line. At the pedestrian crossing soon reached, cross over to Aqueduct Street, cross the road to a small parkland area on the left and up to the present terminus of the canal, a mile from Preston station. The aqueduct, which was a small one similar in design to others that will be seen later, has long since been demolished. Looking back towards the station the original line of the canal can partly be determined, but there are sadly few signs left of its existence. (Note that buses from Preston bus station pass down Fylde Road, should you prefer not to walk.)

A finger post at the end of the canal tells, amongst other distances, 41¼ miles to Tewitfield and 57 miles to Kendal. A few yards along the towpath there is bridge number 10 (bridges 1 to 8 are on the Glasson Arm; there is no Bridge 9) which takes the path over the entrance to the Ashton Basin, the original basin at Preston. From here both sides of the canal, which is in a cutting for half a mil e, are lined with houses, gardens on the offside leading down to the water. Bridge 11 is the first bridge over the canal and has been much widened. Next is Bridge 11a taking Blackpool Road over the canal; formerly an ugly structure, but now replaced with a much more attractive bridge of concrete sections. By Bridge 12, Woodplumpton Road, Haslam Park appears on the left, a pleasant spot easily reached from the towpath. Water from the canal is taken off here to flow into Savick Brook. From in the park, Bridge 13, Savick Aqueduct, the first aqueduct, can be seen taking the canal over Savick Brook whose waters form the basis of the Millennium Ribble Link.

Back on the towpath Bridge 14, Hollinghead Fold, is the first of many Rennie 'standard' bridges spanning the canal. On the off side of the canal the 2 miles from Preston milestone is in a garden. Just beyond is Bridge 15, Ingol Ashes, another Rennie standard, but with a pointed parapet rather than a curved one and it is topped with rails. The next bridge, 16, Cottam Mill, is similar but without the rails. From here the canal becomes gradually more rural as the city is left behind. A few yards further on the towpath crosses over the junction of the Millennium Ribble Link with the main line.

Bridge 15, Ingol Ashes

Angling at Salwick Wharf

A new bridge, 16A has a winding hole (where longer boats can be turned) by it and carries the B6241, Tom Benson Way, over the canal. From here onwards the busy railway line to Blackpool is close to the canal which now heads out for the Fylde Plain, coming within 2 miles of Kirkham.

Bridge 17, Cottam Hall, is a skew Rennie standard, not a common type on the Lancaster Canal as most are at 90 degrees to the water channel. On the off side around new housing development the side of the canal is landscaped and includes a walk and a small play area for children. There is a pier and a signpost stating 'LANCASTER CANAL, Tewitfield 40 miles, Preston 2½ miles'.

At Bridge 18, Lea Malt Kiln, Lea Road crosses the canal.

From Bridge 19, Harrisons or Quakers, to Bridge 25 is part of the Westinghouse Emergency Planning Zone. The siren, which is continuous like an air raid siren, is tested for two minutes at 14.00 on the first Tuesday of February, May, August and November. If it is heard outside these times, pedestrians should leave the area immediately. Boat users should shut themselves in their vessels, closing all doors, windows, etc. and turn off heating, air conditioning and ventilation systems.

Beyond Bridge 19, just before reaching the double pylon line, there was Lea Swing Bridge (Bridge number 20), one of only three swing bridges on the canal. Sadly it fell into bad condition and was removed several years ago, so only the masonry on either side of the water channel, which is narrower at this point, remains. The bridge served farmland.

Bridge 23, Wards House, is the first one to still have stop planks by it, these being on the off side. These are to be found by many bridges along the canal and are for dropping down a slot in the stonework so as to dam the canal at either end of a leak. There are also stop planks at Bridge 24, Salwick Hall. The Hall is not open to the public.

Salwick is better known for British Nuclear Fuels Springfields plant than for the canal, only a few yards away. Bridge 25, Wilson's, is close to Salwick station which most trains pass straight through on their way to Preston or Blackpool. By leaving the canal at Bridge 25, going down to the road and turning left, passing Salwick station and then Springfields, Clifton is reached from where there are regular buses to Preston and Kirkham and beyond.

From Bridge 25 the canal turns north. The moorings here were Salwick Wharf which was the nearest point to the market town of Kirkham. It was once projected that a canal would serve Kirkham and the Fylde from this stretch of the Lancaster Canal, which is the reason for the large loop into this area, but nothing came of it. For the next half mile the canal passes through the attractive tree-lined Salwick Cutting. Bridge 26, Kirkham or Salwick Bridge, is a skew standard which is deeper than normal to accommodate the depth of the cutting. It carries a minor road from Salwick or Kirkham to Woodplumpton or the north of Preston. By it is the Hand and Dagger pub. The cutting ends at Bridge 27, Marshalls or Six Mile. Close by is a milestone indicating it is six miles from Preston. The canal continues northwards to Bridge 28, Salwick Moss or New Bridge, as it is shown on some maps. The latter name is from when the present bridge replaced a lift bridge. Once under the M55 motorway (Bridge 28a), come to Bridge 29, Kellet's or Fletcher's Bridge, and the canal then turns eastwards again, away from the Fylde Plain. Here four of the many radio masts of *RNWS Inskip* are a dominant feature out on the Fylde Plain. It is a communications centre for the Ministry of Defence. Blackleach Marina is passed on the offside. Bridge 31, Stone Chimney, is another Rennie standard which has pointed parapets, but is the only such bridge which is skew. Immediately before Bridge 32, Swillbrook,

Salwick Wharf

Marshalls or Six Mile Bridge

Reeds with Moons Bridge Marina, near bridge 36

Hollowforth Swing Bridge, number 37

near Catforth is the milestone showing 8 miles from Preston. Beyond the bridge are the former canal stables and cottages. These have been tastefully converted to housing. Here, are Pendle Marine, Bumbles and Canal Boat Escapes and a slip where boats can be launched into the canal.

Beyond Catforth the canal crosses Woodplumpton Brook by a small uninteresting aqueduct, Bridge 33. By Bridge 34, Winneyfield, are stop planks. Woodplumpton village is easily reached from either Bridge 35, Bell Fold, or Bridge 36. By the skew Bridge 36, Moons Bridge, is Moons Bridge Marina.

Hollowforth Swing Bridge, 37, is one of only two now left on the canal. The original bridge was constructed of wood and had two vertical wooden posts on the offside to which were fastened the iron tension rods which supported the crossbeams that carried the roadway. It has been replaced by a modern bridge. The bridge swings on ball-bearings which are on a circular race between the stone foundations. It serves farmland on the opposite side of the canal from the farm passed here.

A few hundred yards further on is the not very well known Hollowforth Aqueduct, Bridge 38. It is possible to sail or walk over it without noticing. It carries the canal over Barton Brook. A hand rail takes a steep path down from the far end of the aqueduct to the brook below. A public footpath to Newsham, about half a mile away, passes under the aqueduct which has three arches, the middle one for the mainstream of the brook and the left for the footpath and some water. The pathway is of metal mesh and passes under the aqueduct just above the water level.

From here, the canal turns northwards for quite a distance. At Bridge 39, Hepgreave Lane, the towpath can be left for a walk of about a mile into Barton from where buses to Garstang and Preston can be caught. The canal passes on through a rural stretch where public footpaths but no roads cross the next two bridges. A road from Bridge 42, White Horse, leads again to the A6 and this time the northern end of Barton.

The canal passes on to Bilsborrow (also shown as Duncombe on some maps), where it is only a few yards to the A6 and the bus services from Bridge 44, Roebuck. By the towpath there is Guy's Thatched Hamlet.

Cattle by the canal near Head Nook Bridge, 42

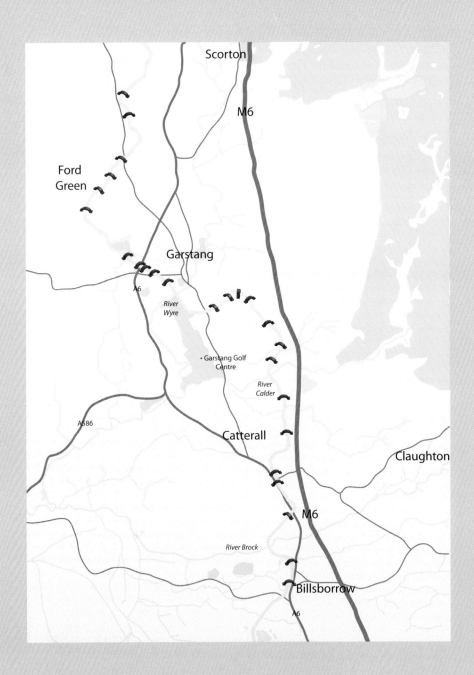

CHAPTER 13

Bilsborrow to Garstang

AT BRIDGE 44, ROEBUCK, by the towpath is Guy's Thatched Hamlet, including a pub and a restaurant. From here, it is an attractive stretch of canal through Bilsborrow with several boats moored along the side of the canal; part of the stretch is tree-lined.

From Bridge 45, Myerscough Bridge, there is a footpath leading to the renowned agricultural college, Myerscough College, with its garden centre and cafe. The road across Bridge 44 also leads to it. Beyond here, the canal swings sharply westwards before crossing the Brock by the first of Rennie's 'little aqueducts' (the others being over the Wyre, the Conder and the Keer). To take the river below the level of the canal to

Along the Lancaster Canal at Bilsborrow

Brock Aqueduct

Crossing Brock Aqueduct

Pisces prepares to sail, Claughton Lane Bridge 49

a sufficient depth to allow for the strong construction of the aqueduct, it was necessary to dig out to a lower level. Above the aqueduct, which is 23 feet above the river, a weir was built to drop the water to a lower level. A few yards before reaching the aqueduct there is a path going to the left and leading down to a good viewpoint for the aqueduct and weir beyond.

At Brock the canal passes beneath the A6 at Bridge 47, Green Man Bridge, named after a building to the right on the A6 which was formerly a public house. From here it is a short walk to the Preston–Garstang bus stops to the right. Close by are Barton Grange Garden Centre and Marina. Beyond the bridge the canal runs up to the railway line and here, only a few yards from it, the A6 road and the M6 motorway. There are views to the Bowland Fells. The canal continues along a pleasantly wooded stretch to Bridge 51, Stubbins, just before which is a house converted from a stable and attendants' accommodation. Bridge 52, Calder Aqueduct, takes the River Calder beneath the canal by means of a syphon. Beyond Bridge 53, Catterall Bridge, is the feeder from the Calder, entering the canal at the basin.

The remains of a windlass near Catterall 53

Bridge 54, Ray Lane, lies by the site of the former Garstang and Catterall station, long since closed and demolished. It was here that the branch line to Pilling and Knott End, the Garstang and Knott End Railway, joined the main line. By the bridge there are two flights of steps up to the road. The broad steps are 'horse stairs' whilst the narrower steps to their right were for the 'horse lad'.

Beyond Bridge 57, Greenhalgh Bridge, the ruins of Greenhalgh Castle are to be seen. The castle was built in 1490 by the Earl of Derby and was a Royalist stronghold in the Civil War. It can be accessed from Bridge 56, Turners.

Now the canal turns south-westwards to Bonds on the outskirts of Garstang, then north-west to Bridge 61, the Wyre Aqueduct. This is the second of Rennie's 'little aqueducts' and has a span of 34 feet. A footpath to Bonds passes beneath. Just beyond lies Garstang basin and then Bridge 62, Kepple Lane, by Th'owd Tithebarn and a convenient spot to leave the canal for buses to Preston, Blackpool or Lancaster. Cross the bridge and go straight ahead to the main street. Turn off left onto Park Hill Road before reaching it for buses to the north. In general, buses to the south pass along Garstang High Street and can be caught at Bridge Street, but not on a Thursday, Market Day, when they are caught on Park Hill Road.

The Wyre Aqueduct 61

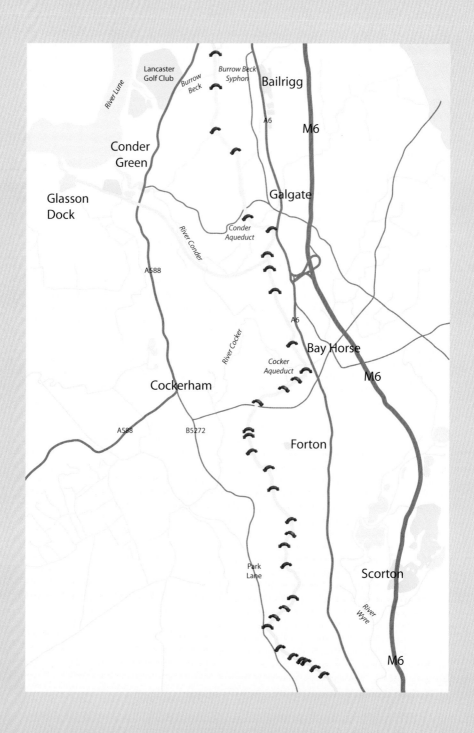

CHAPTER 14

Garstang to Galgate

G ARSTANG IS A PLEASANT small market town (market day Thursday) and the first 'Fair Trade Town' in the world. To reach the canal basin from Bridge Street, go up to the Square and turn left down Church Street, passing St Thomas' Church. Cross over Park Hill Road. On the left, just before the bridge, is the entrance to Th'owd Tithebarn, now a restaurant. The building is over a century older than the canal and stands on the north side of the basin. Unusually for the time, it is built of brick.

From Bridge 62, Keppel Lane, beside the basin, the canal skirts Garstang. Bridge 63a, Water Pipe, carries a pipe taking water to Blackpool and the Fylde from Barnacre Reservoir. Inscribed with the legend 'FWB 1927', it has a long, narrow arch, but does not take pedestrians.

From Garstang to Galgate the canal is never far from the A6 and buses to Lancaster or Garstang. Bridge 63b, A6, takes the canal under that road. This is followed by Bridge 64, Cathouse, from where the canal generally takes on a rural aspect all the way to Lancaster. On the offside is Bridge House Marina which has its own separate entrance and exit from the main line of the canal. A few yards further north-west are the remains of the 'Pilling Pig', as the Garstang and Knott End Railway was known. The tracks have long since been removed and the bridge itself demolished, but the brickwork of the support remains by the towpath. The bridge was number 65. By it is Garstang Marina.

Just before reaching Bridge 66, Nateby Hall Bridge, the canal turns northwards towards Cabus. Bridge 71, Winmarleigh, lies about a mile east of the hamlet of that name. There are now views of the Bowland Fells to the east and across flat, open country to the west. Just before reaching Bridge 75, Ratcliffe, there are Ratcliffe Wharf moorings on the offside. These are long term moorings. Once, the wharf was busy with canal barges. Behind the moorings there are mounds to be seen, these

Autumn near Corless Bridge 76

Corless Bridge 76

Bridge 77 Smiths

being the tops of lime kilns. Barges brought limestone for burning and coal for the burning process. The burnt lime was used on improving the farmland and to make mortar. By leaving the towpath at the bridge and going right along Ratcliffe Wharf Lane for a short distance, the front of one of the kilns can be seen, but it is bricked up. It can also be seen that the canal is higher than the bottom of the kiln. This would make loading the kiln from the top much easier. The 1817 list of canal rentals shows that A Whitehead rented just over an acre of land here for £1 1s. 0d. a year for twenty one years from 1 January 1801. This included 'Lime Kilns and Wharf'.

There are several Rennie standard bridges with variations on the following stretch. Bridge 78, Stony Lane, is railed because during the last war the parapet was taken down to the string course so that any enemy troops would be seen crossing the bridge! Bridge 80, Richmond, is pointed. There are several typical canalside woodlands along here, making it a most pleasant stretch.

Bridge 79 Cockerham Road

Shortly before reaching Stony Lane Bridge, Clifton Hill is seen on the right, back in the 1880s the home of Mrs Catherine Mary Fitzherbert Brockholes, a widow. It has now been divided into separate dwellings. About a quarter of a mile beyond the bridge the canal narrows and some masonry work can be seen by the water. This was the site of Clifton Hill Bridge. On 7 December 1888, Mrs Fitzherbert Brockholes and Charles Henry Bird, presumably a farmer on the adjacent land, released to the London and North Western Railway Company, the then owners of the Lancaster Canal, 'All rights of way and passage whatsoever over across or upon the Bridge called Clifton Hill Bridge …' They also covenanted that the Railway Company might at any time remove the bridge. An examination of the site and of the plan with the deeds suggests that the bridge was actually a lift bridge and not a stone bridge.

At Bridge 81, Potters Brook, the canal is very close to the A6 with bus stops just to the right. Just beyond is the site of Bay Horse Station which was the scene of the rail crash on 21 August 1848 (see Chapter 5). Bridge

Bridge 84 Ellel Grange

82 is a small aqueduct taking the canal over the River Cocker, a very small river. By Bridge 83, Hay Carr, there are private moorings. Beyond here the canal passes through the private estate of Ellel Grange. Bridge 84, Ellel Grange, takes the driveway from the main road and is the only Rennie standard bridge with a pierced parapet with balusters, this being done to suit the setting.

Double Bridge, 85, is a standard of double width. It serves two farms, was built on their boundary and so is divided by a wall down the middle. A few yards beyond this is bridge number 1, Junction Bridge, taking the towpath over the junction of the Glasson Dock Arm. It is a turnover bridge, so constructed that horses did not need be disconnected from the boats. Whilst of similar appearance to a Rennie standard, it obviously could not have been built until around 1825 when the Glasson Arm was under construction. By the bridge is the lock-keeper's cottage. On the offside, a little further along, there are extensive moorings terminating in Galgate Marina. At Bridge 86, Galgate, the towpath can be left and turn right to the main road. Bus stops are either side of the road here. The village of Galgate is reached by turning left.

The former Lockkeeper's Cottage at Galgate

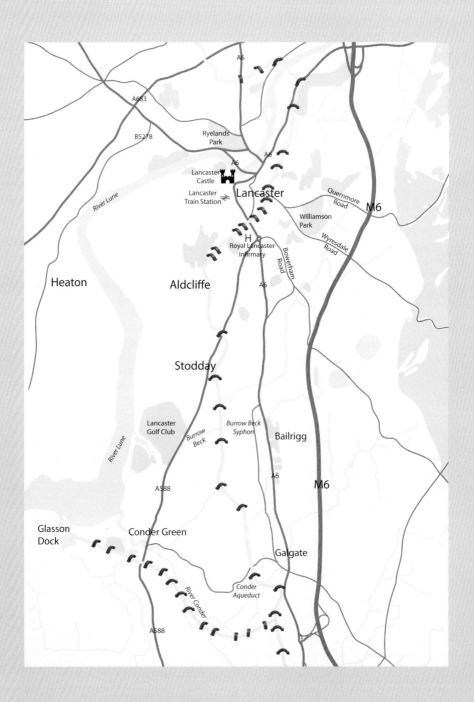

CHAPTER 15

Galgate to Lancaster

THE BEST POINT AT WHICH to join the canal towpath is from by the Plough Inn bus stop, just to the south of the huge railway viaduct which dominates the village. Go down the lane by Galgate Marina to Bridge 86, Galgate, and onto the towpath and turn left.

Bridge 87 is the third of Rennie's 'little aqueducts' and carries the canal across the River Conder. This aqueduct has buttresses and wing walls on either side and a low segmental arch (there being no path beneath) above which is a curved retaining wall.

Just over a mile further north at Bridge 91, Brantbeck Bridge, is the start of Deep Cutting. This cutting is roughly 1.5 miles in length and

The Conder Aqueduct 87

Reflections at Galgate

Burrow Beck syphon

ends just beyond Bridge 94, Ashton Lane Bridge, which carries the A585 from Lancaster. The cutting is lined with trees and most attractive, in the autumn especially. Part of the bed of the canal is cut into solid rock and is not lined. About a quarter of a mile into the cutting is the second of the two syphons on the Lancaster Canal. It is much easier to see this syphon's way of working than the Calder one's since it is more accessible and the canal is narrower here. In 1794, whilst the canal was being cut though this stretch, the navvies unearthed a major find of the Roman occupation. It consisted of seven stone sculptures: two lions, four heads and one of the goddess Ceres. The stones, now housed in the Lancaster City Museum, had apparently been buried in a pit and it seems likely that they came from a family mausoleum of an important Romanised native of the district. Within the cutting is Bridge 93, Carr Lane also popularly known as 'Broken Back Bridge', probably because the roadway dips to the centre instead of being humpbacked.

As the cutting is left behind, Lancaster Castle can be seen ahead. Here was known to bargees as 'Hangman's Corner' as condemned prisoners

Carr Lane or Broken Back Bridge

were said to have been exercised here. A short way on, a second path runs parallel to the towpath itself on the same side of the canal. Before reaching Aldcliffe Road the canal passes through another, shallower, cutting while the second path passes along the top before dropping down to join the towpath again at the road. The canal turns sharply right at Aldcliffe Road. The following stretch is the only length of the canal where towpath and road are immediately adjacent, with only a fence between them, and formerly not even that.

Bridge 95, Haverbreaks, is the only standard bridge with no keystone in the arch. Bridge 96, Aldcliffe Road Footbridge, was a ship's gangway that replaced an old pitch pine bridge in May 1954. Originally the gangway was 90 feet in length, but the central 36 feet had to be cut away to fit in across the stone supports. In the road side of the bridge there is a post box; the only one in a bridge on the Lancaster Canal. The present box replaces an earlier one.

The main railway line, formerly the line joining the Lancaster and Preston Junction Railway, crosses the canal at Bridge 97. Just beyond the bridge, on the offside, is a two-storey building. It is the Boat House where the packet boats were repaired. It had for many years been in a ruinous state and there had been a proposal that it be demolished, but it was rejected by the planning committee of Lancaster City Council and was restored in the 1990s. The boats, which were long and thin, were raised by pulleys on the beams of the upper floor. The front of the building is skewed to allow for the launching of these boats. Now, where the boats once entered are balconies, the building having been converted into two apartments. This was as a part of a larger scheme which included the building of houses on the former BWB yard and the conversion of the workshops to housing.

Beyond here was the British Waterways Board yard and there were often work boats about. Now, it too has been converted to housing, but the crane remains.

By the towpath, opposite the former yard, is what is known as the Aldcliffe Road Triangle. This land is owned by the Canal and River Trust but leased to Lancaster City Council until 2070. Formerly, it was a repair

Along Deep Cutting, looking southwards

Former boathouse, Lancaster, before and after conversion

yard for punts, having once been a sandpit according to the 1846 OS map and later the yard of Joe Johnson, a paving contractor. A local community group, the Fairfield Residents' Association, has been sublet the area by Lancaster City Council and has cleared the site, made various repairs and lowered the wall by the towpath. It is now an attractive amenity area.

The BWB yard was reached from Bridge 98, a turnover bridge which is often known as Fox's Bridge but also known as Basin Bridge. Horses could be backed over the bridge without being disconnected from their boats. From here, for a short stretch, the towpath is on the right-hand side of the canal. At the end of the bridge are the recently converted former canal workshops that are now living accommodation.

Beyond the bridge are two large basins where barges were loaded and unloaded, now surrounded by student accommodation, and then a paved area with seating where the Lancaster Canal Company's offices were sited. Opposite, on the towpath side, is the 'Waterwitch', a public house in the former stables which have been converted and extended. For a while, punts for sailing on the canal could be hired from the stables before their extension and conversion.

The footbridge by the Waterwitch was erected for people to cross to the pub from the car park on Aldcliffe Road. It was lowered into place on 12 January 1987; a bitterly cold day when the canal was frozen over. The workmen were able to walk across the ice!

Next is Bridge 99, Penny Street Bridge, from which it is only a short walk to the left to the town centre. It is much widened from its original form. To the right you will find that buses stop for various parts of the town, for Morecambe, Preston, Garstang and Blackpool. A few yards along the road, past the main Royal Lancaster Infirmary gate, a building which has been a nurses' home and is now offices to the Infirmary, is facing down the road. This was the Lancaster and Preston Junction Railway's station and terminus of their line.

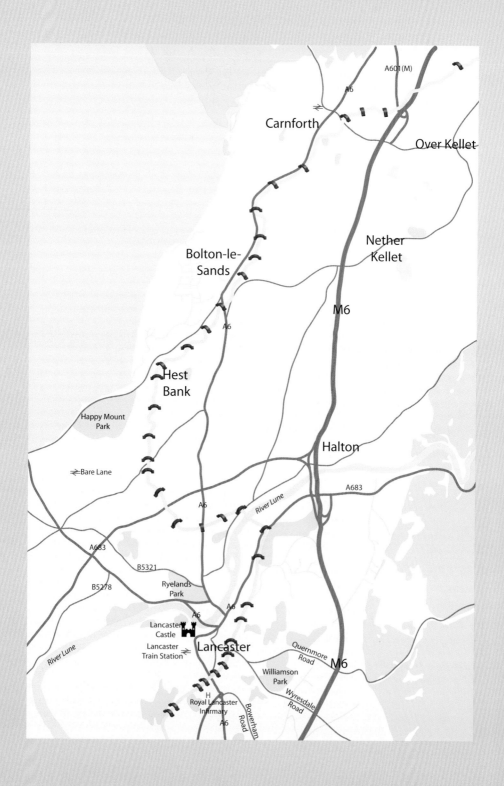

CHAPTER 16

Lancaster to Carnforth

THE TOWPATH CAN BE REACHED from either the Lancaster Infirmary side, or the White Cross side of the road at Penny Street Bridge. White Cross was White Cross Mills, but they are now closed as mills, partly demolished, and the remainder occupied by various businesses. There were several mills alongside the canal in Lancaster, Moor Lane Mills, Bath Mills and Albion Mills to name but three; all having been demolished or converted for other uses.

The 1846 Ordnance Survey map shows that the Packet Boat Station was close by Penny Street Bridge on the White Cross side.

At Bridge 100, Friarage Bridge, the canal towpath crosses back again to the left-hand side. The original bridge has been replaced by a modern one and the area around it landscaped. Towering above the canal is St Peter's, the Roman Catholic cathedral, perhaps the finest work of local architects Paley & Austin. Bridge 101, Nelson Street, bears the legend 'Joseph Clayton, 1876' and is a skew bridge which takes the road to the Trough of Bowland across the canal. Presumably it was Joseph Clayton who widened the bridge. Former mills stand by Bridge 102, Moor Lane Bridge. The next bridge is 103, Dry Dock. For a small diversion, turn left into Shaw Street, which has old stone flags for the pavement, and go up the steps, across the bridge, and turn left along the road. Continue along Sylvester Street and come to a quite high stone wall. At the end of the wall there is a good viewing point for the old graving dock and its junction with the main line of the canal.

From the graving dock, either continue along the street to Bridge 104, Ridge Lane, to regain the towpath or return to it via Shaw Street. If doing the latter, after passing under the bridge, Dry Dock is seen as it is passed, but nowhere near so clearly. The canal passes on through a residential part of Lancaster to a large embankment with a small stream below. Across the canal to the right there is a golf course, beside which the canal turns sharply north-west.

It now approaches the Bulk Aqueduct, also known as Caton Road Aqueduct, across the A683 to Yorkshire. This modern concrete replacement of a stone aqueduct by Rennie enabled the road to be widened in 1961. For 12 months, while the work went on, boats had to be lifted from the water and transported on a cradle and carriage along the gantry to the other side. Nearly 300 boats were transferred in this manner. Close by the aqueduct, on private land adjacent to the golf course, are the remains of coke ovens, but these can only be glimpsed when there is no foliage to obscure them.

This aqueduct is followed by a huge embankment. A leak in the bed caused this section of the canal to be closed and drained for several weeks from June 2015. To keep the canal on the Preston side of the leak in water, a pipe was laid from by the Halton Road Bridge, across the aqueducts, and to a dam by the golf course, water being pumped through it.

Lune aqueduct floodlit 29 Oct 2013

Lune Aqueduct, eastern side

Next, the highlight of the canal, the magnificent Lune Aqueduct. This is best seen from below and the river banks can be easily reached from the towpath. Riverside footpaths to Halton and Lancaster pass below the aqueduct and its size and structure is best appreciated from them. The former Skipton to Morecambe railway line passed beneath the southern end of the aqueduct, its line now being one of the paths.

Just before reaching Halton Road Bridge 108, there is a small basin on the offside. By it there is an overflow outlet to the Lune and the steady pour of water can be heard. Aqueduct Cottage, long since demolished, stood immediately to the north of the bridge by the towpath. After passing under the bridge the canal turns sharply to the south-west, passing houses on the outskirts of Lancaster. At Beaumont Turnpike, bridge number 110, the canal passes under the A6, the bridge being a

Working on balustrading, Lune Aqueduct

Lune Aqueduct drained 9 July 2015

Firming new clay, leak at Lancaster, July 2015

much widened standard. Bus stops to Lancaster or Carnforth are close by. Bridge 111, Hammerton Hall Bridge, takes a minor road back, past St John's Hospice, to Beaumont Bridge. Hammerton Hall Farm is passed on the right and then the canal turns north-west to what was open country. However, all this area changed with a new bridge, 111a, Milestone Bridge, over the canal, carrying the link road between the M6 and Heysham, the Bay Gateway. Bridge 112 is Folley Bridge, but the farm is now called Foley Farm, one 'l' having been dropped! Bridge 114, Belmount Bridge, is sometimes known as Skew Bridge although it is actually the road which is skew, not the bridge. Most bridges are straight across the canal, the roads having been angled. Bridge 115, Blind Lane Bridge, is at the end of a narrow lane which led down to Belmount Cottage and stables, most traces of which have now vanished. We are now 4 miles from Lancaster.

Hilda Robinson was born at Belmount Cottage in 1925 to William Bewes, the canal ranger, and his wife Isabel. In 2004, she told how the living accommodation was at one end, a large wash-house in the centre and the stables at the other end. Above the stables were haylofts. There was no

Milestone Bridge under construction

Milestone Bridge

running water or electricity. Coal barges stayed there overnight to rest the horses. The boatmen enjoyed listening to their hosts' gramophone. Hilda's parents left the cottage in 1953.

In about half a mile Hest Bank is reached, the closest the canal comes to the sea. The Hest Bank Hotel is handy for buses for Lancaster and Carnforth, while a walk down towards the shore leads also to bus stops for Morecambe and Carnforth. Goods brought by sea to Hest Bank Pier, which was built in 1820, were transferred to canal boats here. This trade dropped off following the opening of the Glasson Branch in 1826. As the canal winds its way from Hest Bank there are good views across Morecambe Bay and towards Warton Crag. Bridge 120, Hatlex Swing Bridge, is the last of the swing bridges, the bridge itself being a comparatively recent replacement. Bridge 121 taking the A6 road over the

Hest Bank Bridge with the former 1820 warehouse on the left, reflected in the still waters.

canal is normally known as Town End Bridge, but can also be known as Mary Huttons. The present bridge replaced a Rennie standard when the by-pass road was built in 1926.

Bridge 122, Bolton Church, can be left so as to go up to the centre of Bolton-le-Sands. By Bridge 123, Bolton Turnpike, there was a Swift Boat service stop and wharf. What was the Packet Boat Hotel stood across the

Hatlex Swing Bridge, snow

Bolton Turnpike Bridge, Bolton-le-Sands

canal close to the former wharf, but it closed in 2015 for conversion to housing. Half a mile beyond, after passing a wood on the right, there is an interesting diversion. One can leave the canal at Bridge 125, Bolton Cinder Ovens, cross over and see where the cinder (coke) ovens were in the field on the left. Continue on down Thwaite Brow Lane to a kissing gate. Pass through this, follow the path down to the canal, through another kissing gate and past the former Cinder Ovens close to Bridge 127, Thwaite End Bridge. This is part of a very old road from Bolton-le-Sands to Carnforth, the Turnpike Road before it was diverted by the coming of the canal. The Friends of Carnforth Coke Ovens have done work trying to find if there are any remains of the ovens at Bolton-le-Sands. At Carnforth, they have worked with the Canal & River Trust clearing the site so that the ovens are now much more exposed and they are hoping to do further work there.

Along the towpath from Bridge 125, there are fine views over Morecambe Bay and to Warton Crag and the north. Just into Carnforth there is the 'Canal Turn' public house, formerly the Canal Company's stables and offices. Opposite, was the large offside marina and also moorings by the former wharf, but it closed on 31 August 2017. This extensive area has been taken over for housing development with a new bridge to span the canal. The canal is only a few yards from the A6 and the bus routes to Morecambe, Lancaster and Kendal. The small industrial estate passed is the site of the former Carnforth gasworks. It is only a short distance from here or the next bridge, 128, Carnforth, and the road down into the centre of Carnforth. Leave the towpath by the playground before reaching the bridge. Trains can be caught from Carnforth station for the Furness district, Yorkshire, Lancaster and the south. The station featured in the famous film 'Brief Encounter' and is now well-known for the Heritage Centre and Refreshment Room.

Chorleys Bridge, Bolton-le-Sands, in winter

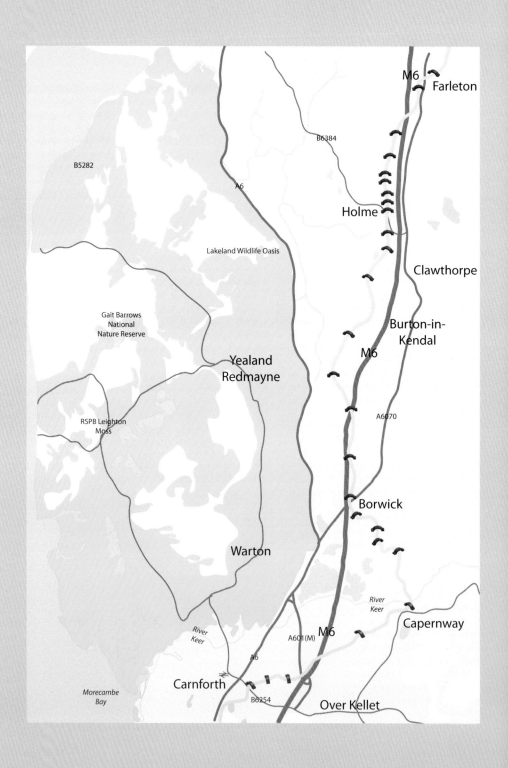

M6
Farleton

B6384

B5282

A6

Lakeland Wildlife Oasis

Holme

Clawthorpe

Gait Barrows
National
Nature Reserve

Burton-in-
Kendal

Yealand
Redmayne

M6

RSPB Leighton
Moss

A6070

Borwick

Warton

River
Keer

Capernway

River
Keer

M6

Morecambe
Bay

River
Keer

A601(M)

A6

Carnforth

B6254

Over Kellet

CHAPTER 17

Carnforth to Tewitfield

REJOIN THE CANAL TOWPATH at either the 'Canal Turn' or at Carnforth Bridge 128. Half way between this bridge and Bridge 129, Hodgsons, there used to be a quarry on the left and stabling for horses used on the canal. Now, all that has been landscaped so that only older residents who lived in the area can remember it. On leaving Carnforth the canal reaches the M6 and Bridge 129a (Brewer's Farm Bridge) leading to junction 35A. Between here and the next bridge, 129b (M6), the canal had to be slightly diverted to the left to make way for part of the motorway junction 35. Bridge 130, Kellet Lane Bridge, is a Rennie standard, and despite its rural location is controlled by traffic lights owing to its blind approaches on both sides.

The canal now runs nearly parallel to the railway line from Carnforth to Skipton as far as Capernwray, where there is a good view of the railway

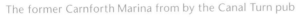

The former Carnforth Marina from by the Canal Turn pub

Kellet Lane Bridge, Carnforth

viaduct from the towpath. At Bridge 131, Capernwray, the towpath can be left and one can drop down the lane to an old pack-horse bridge. The former Capernwray Mill, the house nearest the canal, can also be seen adjacent to the last of Rennie's 'little aqueducts' which takes the canal across the River Keer. This aqueduct is quite narrow as the river passes under the canal at the bottom of a steep-sided valley.

From Bridge 131, Capernwray, there is a path on the offside which leads past the caravan site and the remains of loading cranes to a short arm of the canal to Webber Quarry, a former limestone quarry. A public footpath continues beyond here to near Borwick.

Leaving Bridge 131 on the towpath, after passing over the aqueduct the canal goes under the railway and then turns north for Borwick. At Bridge 135, Borwick Hall, the canal can be left for a look at this

Lancaster Canal near Capernwray

attractive little village. Borwick Hall is Elizabethan and had a pele
tower around which it was built.

From Borwick Hall Bridge the canal quickly passes beneath two more
standard bridges, 136, Sanders, and 137, Taylors, before bending sharp
left for Bridge 138, Tewitfield Turnpike. A short distance beyond lies
Tewitfield Marina and then comes Tewitfield basin and the terminus of
the main cruising section of the canal. Sadly, a good example of a skew
bridge was removed here and the canal culverted under the A6070. The
roadway used from by the canal terminus to the Longlands hotel is the
remains of the original A6070 leading from the demolished bridge. There
is an hourly bus service from Tewitfield, by the Longlands Hotel to
Carnforth and Lancaster or from across the road to Kendal via Burton,
Holme and Milnthorpe.

If the road is crossed to the Kendal side, the canal and the M6 can be
crossed and then a lane to the right. Just beyond the lane, by looking into
the field, a line of trees can be seen, not far from the field wall. Look at
the ground along there and it will be seen that it is the remains of a water
channel, believed to be an abandoned beginning of the authorised branch
to Warton.

Sanders and Taylors Bridges

By the wharf, New England. The bridge carries the railway line to Skipton over the canal

Angling at end of Capernwray Quarry Arm

Tewitfield Marina nearing completion, from opposite its entrance from the main line of the canal

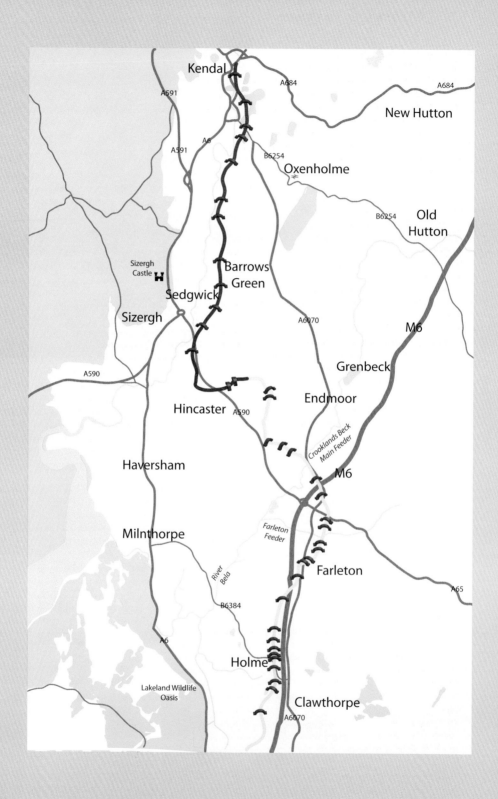

CHAPTER 18

Tewitfield to Holme

ACROSS THE A6070 AT TEWITFIELD lie the remains of the flight of eight locks which raised the canal 76 feet in three-quarters of a mile. A good view of them can be had from the road above. For several years after closure the locks remained complete, the gates and sluices being left open. However, the large wooden gates have now been removed and the locks weired. The tail bridges have been removed and small service bridges put across the top and bottom locks. The masonry of the locks is still in good condition, two hundred years after they were built, and they could be restored, although the making of new gates could be expensive. Lock 4 and the adjacent Lark Bridge, 140, were restored by volunteers in 1992. So as to take small sea-going vessels en route from Glasson to Kendal, the locks were built as wide locks with two gates. Nowadays the M6 runs by, parallel with the flight until the canal turns to the left just beyond Saltermire Bridge beyond the top lock. A canal

The former Tewitfield Locks and the M6 from the bridge on the A6070

Lark Bridge and lock 4

cottage stood by the top lock, but it has long been demolished. It is now necessary to leave the towpath and walk up the road for a few yards before rejoining the canal at Cinderbarrow, the first culvert under the M6 and the point where the top lock must be removed if the canal is restored through to Kendal.

From Cinderbarrow the canal approaches the railway and runs above it (in one part well above) for over half a mile. From here, the canal still has water in the channel, but not to its original depth and it is sometimes culverted, to Stainton which is about seven miles further on. It leaves the main railway line and turns towards Burton. The old Burton wharf is on the offside, just by it Bridge 144, Burton Aqueduct, takes the canal over the road to the former Burton and Holme station. The aqueduct is not visible from above, only from the road. (By passing under the aqueduct and going up the road, the centre of Burton can be reached.) It has a shallow archway over sides which slope slightly outwards from road level. From Burton the towpath is a public right of way (which it is not up to here) through to Kendal.

Nearer Holme there is another aqueduct with a more curved arch, Bridge 145, New Mill Aqueduct, the road beneath joining the road from Burton. There is no official access to the road from the towpath. The canal then passes Holme Mills, a factory colony complete with mill pond and workers' houses. A flour mill had been established here by 1790, before the canal was built. Holme Mills were perhaps the earliest mills in rural Westmorland to use steam power (*circa* 1818). They were rebuilt around 1860, after a fire. The site has now been split into small industrial units. The mill chimney was demolished in September 1983.

Roughly mid way between Bridge 148, Sheernest, and Bridge 149, Holme Turnpike, a bank of cinder ovens is to be seen in a field on the other side of the canal.

Remains of lock mechinism, Tewitfield

Remains of lock gates, Tewitfield

From Holme Turnpike Bridge, which is a skew bridge, it is a short walk into the village of Holme. It seems probable that the Westmorland bridges were an adaptation by Fletcher of Rennie's standard bridge designs, there being a great similarity. This bridge or the previous one are both convenient places to leave the canal for buses for Lancaster or Kendal.

14 miles from Lancaster and Moss Bridge

Holme Mills

CHAPTER 19

Holme to Hincaster

F<small>ROM CLOSE BY</small> H<small>OLME</small> T<small>URNPIKE</small> B<small>RIDGE</small> the bed of the canal is a concrete flume replacing the pipes, mentioned earlier, which had been installed in case of leakages in the canal bed. The canal around Holme is popular with canoeists and there are more bridges there than anywhere else on the canal – eight in a mile (the last now being a culvert).

Dominating the canal at this point is Farleton Fell, a limestone crag which has been extensively quarried. Shortly after leaving Holme the canal is once again culverted. The walker has to leave the towpath, pass along the edge of the field by the motorway, then come out by the bridge carrying the Farleton to Milnthorpe road over the M6 which is then crossed to Bridge 155, Duke's Bridge. The residence opposite is a former

Holme Turnpike Bridge

coaching inn dating back to 1630, and after which the bridge is named, and it in turn was named after the Duke of Somerset. The bridge is unusual in that there is an archway in the offside to allow livestock to pass through. To the right the towpath goes back to the culvert, passing a very well preserved milestone on the way.

After passing under the bridge the remains of a disused stable and packet house is reached. Attempts to have this building restored failed a number of years ago. Opposite is the Farleton winding hole where boats

Duke's
Bridge,
Farleton

Winding Hole and remains of stables, Farleton

were turned. Four more bridges are passed in quick succession. Shortly after leaving Farleton there is an outlet to Lupton Beck on the towpath side. Just beyond here is a minor feeder from Lupton Beck which brings water down from Wyndhammere, an artificial tarn near Mansergh. A few hundred yards further on, past Dovehouse's Bridge, 161, the A675 crosses the canal on an embankment, the canal being culverted at 162, Moss Side Culvert. The towpath passes beneath the road bridge which, if it had been made a little wider, could have taken a water channel making it accessible to cruising boats.

In another half mile the next culvert is reached at Millness near to Crooklands, where it is necessary to leave the canal, walk under the M6 and rejoin the towpath on the other side. Beyond the next bridge, 164, Millness, the canal reaches Crooklands where there is the main feeder, the water being brought down from Killington Reservoir via Peasey Beck (also known as Crooklands Beck). The beck passes beneath the canal a few yards up from the feeder. By leaving the towpath and following the road back for a few yards, Crooklands Aqueduct, 165, can be seen.

Coke manufacture used to be carried out at Crooklands. By 1819 Earl

Balcarres, a Wigan coal-owner and one of the canal's proprietors had a long wharf and several coke ovens there. There is still a coal merchant's yard.

Bridge 166, Crooklands, carries heavy traffic, something for which it was not originally designed. By it, on the towpath side is a large buttress which once carried a wagonway for bringing gunpowder down from Gatebeck works to the canal at Wakefield's Wharf. The other buttress is several yards away, making for the canal being crossed at an angle.

Crooklands
Stable

Old Hall Bridge, 167, Crooklands

Plate against rope rubbing on Mattinsons Bridge

Later, a line was laid down to the railway station and its site can still be seen in the broad verge to the road. The former stables, by the towpath, have been restored by the Lancaster Canal Trust and a picnic area created. The Trust's cruise boat, *Waterwitch*, is normally moored opposite and she takes passengers for trips along the canal on Sundays and Bank Holidays plus some other dates during the summer. Just beyond is Wakefield's Wharf, built to service the traffic from Wakefield's gunpowder works. It is not known for certain, but thought that the stable was built specifically for the horses which worked Wakefield's gunpowder boats. It would be built at a distance from the wharf to avoid the risk of a spark from a horse's shoes whilst boats were being loaded.

From Crooklands the canal turns westwards, past a long line of conifers, and then northwards again at Bridge 168, Mattinson's Bridge, the second one after leaving Crooklands. Beyond here, on the offside, is the '7 miles from Kendal' milestone. At Bridge 169, Field End Bridge, the canal turns north-west and, a little further on, west. Here is Stainton Beck, another minor feeder, the water being brought down Saint Sunday's Beck (the name changes at Stainton). Further downstream this Beck becomes the River Bela into which Crooklands Beck also flows.

Stainton Beck passes beneath the canal which is carried on a small, attractive skew aqueduct designed by Thomas Fletcher and which is Grade II listed. A footpath passes under the aqueduct alongside the stream, and can be reached by steps down from the towpath. This aqueduct was very badly damaged as a result of Storm Desmond in

Working on the towpath and canal bed, Stainton

December 2015. The stream is normally very shallow, but the severity of the storm caused it to rise by six or seven feet above normal. The turbulence of the water caused the scouring of the bed of the beck and resulted in the washing away of the path and part of the embankment. This led to the undermining of the foundations of the south-west wing wall which subsided and rotated, so breaking the arch of the Aqueduct. This resulted in the closure of the canal towpath and temporary repair work having to be done to strengthen the damaged structure so as to prevent further movement and enable the reopening of the towpath again. A bund was put across the bed of the canal a few yards below the aqueduct and the water level then reduced so as to reduce pressure on the aqueduct. The water was pumped out into the 'First Furlong' and then overflowed from there into the 'Second Furlong'.

At the time of writing, it is hoped that full repairs will be completed in time for the Canal's bicentenary celebrations in 2019.

A few hundred yards further on, beneath Bridge 172, Stainton Crossing, the official end of the watered section is reached, the canal being stopped at the time of writing. Up to this point the canal is the responsibility of the Canal and River Trust. Beyond, it is the responsibility of Cumbria County Council.

Stainton Crossing Bridge after much clearance work had been done on the
First Furlong

Beyond Stainton Crossing Bridge, where an earthen dam marks the end
of the watered section, the Lancaster Canal Trust has done much work
on what is known as 'First Furlong'. The bed of the canal was empty of
water for many years and had become very overgrown. The towpath was
in very poor condition.

The Lancaster Canal Trust volunteers and Waterways Recovery Group
work parties have done much work felling trees where necessary, removing
all the undergrowth and excavating the canal bed up to Bridge 173, Sellet
Hall. The towpath has been re-instated. In 2014 the canal bed was relined
and it was hoped to remove the bund and reconnect with the canal.
Unfortunately, the material used for relining proved to be unsatisfactory
and leaked. After much consideration by the Trust, a new lining was
settled upon. However, first the failed lining had to be removed together
with all the earth and mud above the original clay.

A new clay bund was put in by Sellet Hall Bridge so that a test could be done for leakage through the wash walls. That short stretch was filled with water and soon proved that it was leaking like a sieve. That has resulted in a lot of pointing having to be done, plugging the stonework with a waterproof lime mortar.

In August 2017, it was finally decided what to do about relining the canal with work to be done in 2018. A waterproof lining has been laid across the water channel, work being done in 50 metre sections. The lining is a black waterproof membrane which is protected by a white geotextile layer on either side. This lining is held in place by 23,940 concrete blocks.

It is hoped that during the bicentenary year of the opening the canal through to Kendal, the first furlong will have been completed to the satisfaction of the Canal and River Trust, and water will pass underneath Stainton Crossing Bridge again, linking the two stretches of canal, original and restored.

Beyond Sellet Hall Bridge the canal still needs restoration work to be done on it, 'Second Furlong'. In less than half a mile it is cut by the A590 and is reached again by passing along Well Heads Lane, under the bridge, then over a stile on the other side of the road. Ahead lies Hincaster Tunnel. The portals were often obscured by extensive growth, but are now regularly cleared. The canal bed is soft and muddy and not to be walked on and people are warned not to walk through the tunnel.

Hincaster Tunnel, 378 yards long, was a place to which boys from Heversham School went for sport. Charles Chandler, who was a pupil there between 1872 and 1879, wrote of those days:

> We fished in the Moss Side brick pond and the canal and caught sand dabs in the bay.
> The canal swarmed with perch and we caught pike by trolling with an 'otter'.
> All the fish we brought home, Rebecca, the cook fried for us. She was a wonderful woman and cooked eggs, mushrooms, and anything else edible we entrusted to her and every boy always got or thought he got his own particular egg, perch or eel. We bought apples from the farms and I remember that in 1872 we got 20 to 30 apples for a penny.

East Portal and horsepath, Hincaster Tunnel

The canal gave us other sport beside fishing. There were always some adventurous boys who were going to swim through the tunnel. I went once with such a party. A bargeman told us that the water in the middle of the tunnel was as cold as ice. He said he had boys of his own and would not like to see one of us drowned. I was never a good swimmer, so on this occasion I kept the clothes of those who swam, and by shouts and yells I encouraged them to persevere in their enterprise. But they all came back to my end of the tunnel chilled and subdued, and their limbs felt like cold putty.

There is no towpath through Hincaster Tunnel and the barges had to be 'legged' through or pulled by hand by means of a fixed rope attached to the side of the tunnel. The horses were taken over the hill by way of a separate horsepath, which is still used by walkers. It starts near the eastern portal of the tunnel, climbs the hill, passes beneath a small, original, accommodation bridge and then the main London–Glasgow railway line by a small tunnel built later. The path then turns right and then left again, passes beneath another original accommodation bridge, and drops down to the Sedgwick–Hincaster road where the towpath is again joined by the western portal of the tunnel and former canal buildings. Both of the tunnel portals are listed structures. The horsepath is unique as it is not part of any road and is a Scheduled Ancient Monument. The path is in railway ownership and not the Canal and River Trust, who own the tunnel. Much restoration work has been done on the path by the Lancaster Canal Trust work parties, together with the assistance of the Waterways Recovery Group and others. The stone wall by the lower horsepath on the eastern side has been rebuilt by volunteers. Other stonework on the horsepath has been repaired from time to time.

Formerly it was possible to look inside the tunnel at the west portal and see both the change from the use of stone to brick for the lining, and to see a loop to which the fixed rope would be attached. However, this is now fenced off for safety.

From the Hincaster wharf, Lythe Valley damsons used to be transported to their destinations to the south.

The canal runs by the Hincaster road for nearly half a mile until it is cut by the A590, this time more so than anywhere else. It is then necessary to walk along the road, the rest of the way to the entrance to Levens Park, close by the River Kent. If leaving the canal here for bus services, follow the famous avenue of oak trees down to where a sign indicates the public footpath nearer the river. Come out of Levens Park at a gate by the bridge. Buses to the south are to be found a few yards to the left. If going northwards or westwards, cross over the road, pass over the bridge, and then turn left a few yards for the bus stop.

Sedgwick from the aqueduct

Sedgwick Aqueduct

CHAPTER 20

Hincaster to Kendal

I F JOINING THE CANAL FROM LEVENS BRIDGE, go through the park, following the path by the River Kent and then along the avenue of oak trees. At the end, join the road from Hincaster. Turn left and cross over the A590 to a 'Public Footpath' sign to Crow Park Bridge, which is at Natland. Go up the slope until a canal bridge can be seen to the left and aim for it. This is Bridge 177, Sedgwick Hill. If walking from the Kendal direction, carry on close to the fence, roughly following the old canal bed, until the ground to the right drops away to a 'V'. The stile is at the bottom of the 'V'. The canal bed was landscaped in 1985, obliterating it into the fields.

From Sedgwick Hill Bridge the former towpath is again followed. On reaching Bridge 178, Sedgwick Aqueduct, one can drop down to the small, attractive village of Sedgwick. From the road it is seen that it is actually a skew aqueduct spanning the narrow road, and that the canal cuts the village in two. The aqueduct is strongly built of stone, very well buttressed and has a stone-lined water channel, and is still owned by Canal and River Trust. The road arch is fairly narrow with the side walls sloping outwards and the top gently curved. It was once proposed that the aqueduct be demolished so as to widen the road. Instead, as a result of protests, the aqueduct is now deservedly a Scheduled Ancient Monument.

Horse Park Bridge

The canal bed remains for a short distance beyond the aqueduct, parts having been made into gardens. Although it is private land there is still a public right of way along this stretch. A stile is crossed into a field and there is a good view towards Kendal from here. The path crosses the landscaped farmland to Bridge 179, Horse Park Bridge, now isolated in the middle of the field and surrounded by trees. Pass under it and go on to a kissing gate by the woodland at Larkrigg Spring. The channel continues for a further stretch through the woodland, after which it is all filled in and largely landscaped.

The next bridge, 180, Larkrigg Hall was very overgrown with ivy and in need of repointing. The ivy has now been removed and the bridge repaired, repointed and repainted round the arch, so it now looks much as it would have done when first constructed. After passing under the bridge, the towpath is fenced off and follows the line of the hedge and crosses fields with views to the outskirts of Kendal. In places cuttings remain to show where the water channel lay (particularly near Helme Lodge). The towpath comes out to Bridge 181, Crow Park, taking Hawes Lane to Natland on the right. On reaching a road, Natland Road, it is crossed, the canal bridge having been demolished. A little further down a line of trees shows where the canal lay. A sign indicates the footpath to Canal Head, a mile away. From here, the bed is sometimes encroached upon by gardens. Bridge 184 is Natland Mill. After crossing Highgate, the canal is very popular with families out for a walk.

Natland Hall Bridge

Natland Mill Bridge

Ahead lies Bridge 186, Kendal Change or Changeline Bridge. Here the towpath crossed to the other side of the water channel for the last half mile to Canal Head. The bridge is now a listed building, and is the only turnover bridge in Cumbria. It had fallen into a poor state of repair, but has now been restored. Beyond Changeline Bridge were the gasworks

Kendal
Changeline
Bridge

Former Canal Ticket Office, Kendal

which helped to keep the canal open in the 1940s. From here, car parks, factory yards, gardens and allotments line the way, some encroaching onto the canal bed, but the towpath continues as a public footpath and cycleway. There is no bridge as the Burton Road is crossed. The next, and last bridge is 187, Kendal Castle, which has been much widened.

The last few hundred yards to the canal terminus is a sad ending. The dramatic finish with Kendal Castle looking down on the canal does not materialise, but a Council Depot and recycling point does, and the terminus itself is built over. Turn left at the road, along Canal Head North where several of the buildings are those erected originally by Kendal Corporation.

By turning right on reaching the road by the river, crossing a footbridge over the Kent and turning left to the end of Blackhall Road and up it, the bus station is reached. Alternatively, turn left, cross Miller Bridge and head up into the town centre of Kendal.

CHAPTER 21

The Glasson Arm

THE GLASSON DOCK ARM of the canal runs from Lodge Hill, near Galgate, to Glasson Dock. It is 2 miles 5 furlongs in length and has a flight of six locks plus the sea-lock. Boats up to 72 feet in length and 14 feet 6 inches width can be taken through the arm. The total fall between Galgate and the dock is 58 feet 3 inches.

At the junction with the main line (see Chapter Thirteen) is the lock-keeper's cottage and a turnover bridge crossing the arm. Junction Bridge is Bridge 1. The cottage was formerly a service tenancy, but was sold in the 1990s. Immediately below the bridge is the first lock in the flight. All six locks are of the same construction and each holds 75,000 gallons of water. The locks are operated by a gate-paddle mechanism which consists

of a toothed rack fixed on the side of, and parallel with the balance arm on the gates which engages with a pinion at the ground end. The mechanism is operated by turning a handle. At the lock end the rack is fixed by a bracket at the top of the paddle arm which moves to and fro in a slot on the side of the balance arm. In operation, as the pinion is turned the rack moves towards either the ground end or the lock end, bringing the paddle arm over and thereby opening the sluice or closing it. The paddles move

Angling by Junction Bridge, Galgate

Cruisers in Lock 1, Glasson Arm

from side to side instead of vertically, as is more usual. Water enters the locks by means of sluices set into the masonry. Each lock has a side weir to take off surplus water and a tail footbridge for access to the offside. The arm is fed from the main line and the River Conder which flows close to the canal at the upper end of Bridge 3.

The locks are now operated by the boaters, who have a key to the locks securing the sluice gates at each lock.

Above the fifth lock there was a channel leading off from the canal down to Thurnham Mill. The Lancaster Canal Company purchased the mill for £1,100 in 1824 in order to get the water rights and divert the millstream into the canal. The present building dates from 1829/30, but there had been a building on the site for many years before that. The mechanism for controlling the flow of water has now virtually vanished from sight as the mill race from above lock 5, which runs along above the canal by the towpath, has been filled in. Until 1976 it was largely intact and in good condition. Thurnham Mill, stands by the sixth lock, the last of the flight. It was originally driven by a water turbine rather than the more usual wheel, with the race running through the building rather than externally. The turbine was removed by W. & J. Pye Ltd, the then owners, around 1970 to provide more space for warehousing. Now the building is The Mill inn, an hotel and restaurant. It has a three-storey stone-built main block with an adjoining kiln on the north-west end. When it was water-powered, water entered the mill on the south-eastern side where some of the control mechanism remained in view for many years, but no longer. It was returned to the canal by a tail race below the bottom lock. The remains of the tail race can still be seen coming out from below the building.

Below Thurnham Mill is Bridge 6, Thurnham Bridge, which takes the Lancaster–Cockerham road over the canal. The Glasson Arm bridges are of a different design from the others, which suggests that they were William Crosley's own work. From Bridge 6 the canal continues in a straight line to the basin. Bridge 8, Brows, is a good example of a skew bridge and is the only one of this type on the arm. Glasson's church, Christ Church Glasson, was not built until 1840, fourteen years after the canal, and lies beside the towpath a few yards from the bridge.

Sea-going vessels with tall masts come up the canal to this point but cannot proceed further owing to the bridges. Many such vessels pass through the sea-lock and into the canal basin, which is several times larger than the dock itself. The canal basin is 14 feet deep and covers 36,000 square yards. Here the Lancaster Canal Company had a five-storey stone warehouse (now demolished) which was capable of handling 1,500 tons of goods at once. The former London and North Western Railway branch line from Lancaster (built in 1883) used to have sidings up to the canal. The station was 300 yards away beside the river. Now the line has been made into a linear park for much of its length to Lancaster and is a pleasant walk up to Conder Green. This can be made into a pleasant short round trip from either Glasson or Conder Green.

On the western side of the basin is a caged weir with a sluice gate to take overflow water from the basin into the dock itself.

The sea-lock can take vessels up to 98 feet in length and 26 feet beam. It is at this lock that the canal ends and the Lancaster Port Commissioners take over all responsibility. The upper pair of gates of the sea-lock are double, one pair facing to the dock and the other to the basin. This was part of an ingenious system to prevent very high tides flowing into the canal basin. The appropriate pair of gates were used depending on which

Sea Lock and
Glasson Dock

was the higher, the sea in the dock or the canal. Watch was kept on tides of 10.1 metres and above, those of 10.3 metres being level with the canal. However, the upper gates have not been in use since around 2010. The Canal & River Trust engineers undertook a report into the operation of the gates, and concluded that they provided little or no protection to Canal & River Trust. A twelve month trial was undertaken and it was found that there were negligible effects both operationally and environmentally. The water in the basin remained predominately fresh with very little saline intrusion. Now, the upper gates are pinned back and the requirement to exercise them monthly has been removed.

The sea-lock is operated by vertical sluices built into the gates, not by a paddle mechanism as in the flight. The gates are opened and closed by chains built into the masonry and are controlled by winding handles on the banks. A swing bridge takes the road between the two parts of Glasson over the lock. This bridge has been constructed so that its appearance is very similar to the original one, but it is electrically operated and the capstan no longer used. The lock gates and sluices are still manually operated. There are now over a thousand vessels passing through the sea-lock in a year, compared with around two hundred ships in the canal's heyday!

After leaving the canal it is well worth taking time to walk around Glasson and the dock. There is usually plenty of activity. Buses to and from Lancaster can be caught here, but they are not very frequent so a check for timings should be made first if one is not using a car. At the time of writing, the same stop is used whether travelling to or from Lancaster. The service was under threat of withdrawal, but has been retained.

CHAPTER 22

Millennium Ribble Link

I‎T IS PROBABLE THAT THE WALKER of the Millennium Ribble Link will start out by walking along the towpath from somewhere in Preston, perhaps close to the terminus or the Ashton Basin. It will then be followed to the bridge spanning the junction with the main line, over it and then turning left to the large holding basin. From there, go straight down by the staircase of three locks. At the top, by lock 1, is where the wooden statue of a naked man and entitled 'Water', which was part of a series entitled 'Gauging the Ripple', stood for the first few years from the opening of the Millennium Ribble Link. It was rather controversial as many people thought that the statue was doing more than just standing there. Now, that art work has been replaced by a new one of a canal boat mounted on a large bracket. It has a boatman at the stern and displays various tools used on the canal.

Dredger and 3 Rise staircase

Lock 7 in March 2011

At the bottom of the flight is the turning basin where boats using the link have to manoeuvre round the sharp bend to pass under the footbridge and Tom Benson Way. They have to go up to the top of the basin and turn right round. It is here that Savick Brook comes down from Haslam Park and becomes a Navigation rather than a canal. The walker passes over the footbridge and goes up to the crossing over Tom Benson Way and then joins the Brook again to go along the walkway under the Fylde railway line. Ahead is Lock 4, which was the first lock to be built. Savick Brook itself flows round to the right, passing down to rejoin the Navigation below the lock. Passing along the path, which is very popular with dog walkers, it is now very hard to believe that all down here was an earthen mess in 2001 when the area was the beginning of the construction of the Link.

Go straight down the path, which is generally by the navigational channel of the Link. There is an obvious diversion as it passes round a church before crossing the road at Leyland Bridge and then following Savick Brook again. Lock 6 is straight in front as it is approached, the path turning left to go round it. If boats are using it, they can be seen directly going into it or coming out, rather than the usual sideways on. A tubular

'Shrimp' enters lock 7

bridge takes the roadway to the golf course over the Brook; the bridge was prefabricated in sections and then put in place. Bridge 8 is a footbridge to the golf course. Next comes Lock 7. Another tubular bridge, number 9 Goodier Bridge, takes a track which is both a cycleway and a public footpath over the Brook just above the holding basin above Lock 8. Lock 8 is, as a signpost by a gate to the next stretch of path proclaims, the end of the footpath. This lock is actually tidal, as is the basin above it, and the waters can be seen coming up the brook as the tide rises, and it would not be possible for vessels to sail under the bridge across the end of the lock at the top of the tide. At times of high tides the lock can flood right over. A rather rough path goes ahead a very short way. By it are pontoons for the use of craft waiting to use lock 8 or having used it and are going down to the sea-lock.

By going down the roadway to the left at Bridge 9, it is but a short distance to Blackpool Road, A583. As the roadway turns right, there is a stile to cross and there turn right and come to a bus stop for buses to Preston centre in a few hundred yards, close to Lea Gate Hotel. There,

Rotating Sea Lock

the very busy road can be crossed. To the right there is a bridge over Savick Brook. However, the best point for seeing the Rotating Sea Lock, 9, is from by the garage. Beyond the lock, Savick Brook winds its way over Lea Marsh for the last half mile to the River Ribble. Boats then turn to sail down the river and cross it to Tarleton and the Leeds and Liverpool Canal or go up it to Preston Marina. At the time of writing, there is no path out over the marsh.

The Link is in use by boats from April to mid-October, but can be walked all year, and work boats may be seen dredging the bed of Savick Brook in the winter months. Cruisers all travel along it more or less together because of the importance of timings at the rotating sea lock, and they all travel in the same direction on a day. Bookings to use the Millennium Ribble Link have to be made in advance and it is advised to make them as early as possible. They only take place when the tides are right and winds not too high, so may be cancelled. Those conditions are:

- a tide level of between 8.5 and 9.6 metres

- winds of up to 4/5 on the Beaufort Scale

- daylight hours and good visibility

- a suitable flow of fresh water flow in Savick Brook

If the Canal & River Trust consider that conditions on the day are not suitable they have the right to cancel the operation. The staircase locks are operated by Canal & River Trust staff as is Lock 9, the rotating sea lock. The boat crews operate the other locks themselves, but the staff may well help out.

Boats coming up the Link have to pass through lock 8 and into the holding basin above. When one suffered a breakdown on Savick Brook, after leaving the River Ribble, it had to be towed by the boat in front until it was in the holding basin.

Select Bibliography

Primary sources

Acts of Parliament (various re Lancaster Canal), Lancaster Library

Cartwright, W., *General Abstract of the Receipts and Expenditures of the Lancaster Canal, from the commencement of the Surveys in the Year 1791, to the 1st December 1798*, document to shareholders, Lancaster Maritime Museum

In Opposition to the Lancaster and Preston Railway Bill, Parliamentary document (Lancashire Record Office, 1837)

Lancaster Canal Correspondence, various files, Lancashire Record Office

Lancaster Canal Navigation, *Report of the Committee at the General Meeting of the Proprietors* (various years), Lancaster Maritime Museum

Ordnance Survey maps (contemporary editions) and other maps

Rennie, J. and Stephens, A., *Specification of the Mason Work of the Aqueduct over the Lune near Lancaster* (1793), handwritten document, Lancaster Maritime Museum

Secondary sources

Ashmore O., *The industrial archaeology of North-west England* (Manchester University Press: Manchester, 1982)

Baines, E., *Lancashire: A new printing of the two volumes of 'History, directory and gazetteer of the County Palatine of Lancaster'* (Augustus M. Kelly: New York, 1968)

Boucher, C. T. G., *John Rennie 1761–1821*, 1st edition (Manchester University Press: Manchester, 1963)

Brayley, E. W. and Britton, J., *The Beauties of England and Wales* (Harris, Longman and Co.: London, 1815)

Curwen, J. F., 'The Lancaster Canal', *Transactions of the Cumberland and Westmorland Antiquarian and Archaeological Society*, 2.17 (1917)

Davies-Shiel, M. and J. D. Marshall, *The Industrial Archaeology of the Lakes Counties*, 2nd edition (Michael Moon: Beckermet, 1977)

Greville, M. D. and G. O. Holt, *The Lancaster and Preston Junction Railway* (David & Charles: Newton Abbot, 1961)

Hadfield, C. and G. Biddle, *The Canals of North West England* (David & Charles: Newton Abbot, 1970)

Harker, R. C.(? or anon.), *A Historiette of the Lancaster Canal*, Lancaster Reference Library

Humber R. D., *Heversham: The Story of a Westmorland School and Village* (Titus Wilson & Son: Kendal, 1968)

Hunt, D., *A History of Preston*, 1st edition (Carnegie Publishing: Lancaster, 1992)

Lancaster Canal Trust, *The Complete Guide to the Lancaster* Canal, sixth edition (Lancaster Canal Trust, 2017)

Lancaster Canal Trust, *50 years on!* (Lancaster Canal Trust, 2013)

Philpotts, R., *Building the Lancaster Canal* (Blackwater Press: London, 2005)

Rigby, J., *The Lancaster Canal in Focus* (Landy Publishing Co.: Blackpool, 2007)

Satchell, J., *Kendal's Canal* (Kendal Civic Society: Kendal, 2001)

Schofield. M. M., *Outlines of an Economic History of Lancaster, Part II: Lancaster from 1800 to 1860* (Lancaster Branch of the Historical Association: Lancaster, 1951)

Tegg, A., *Lune Aqueduct, Lancaster Canal Conservation Management Plan* (British Waterways Technical Group: 2010)

Periodicals

Lancaster Gazette (various issues)

Lancaster Guardian (various issues)

Lancaster Observer (various issues)

Waterwitch, (Lancaster Canal Trust, various issues available online, https://www.lctrust.co.uk/the-trust/waterwitch-magazine)

Westmorland Gazette (various issues)